ashes left to linger:

a poetic search for closure

by
Sophie Soil

PublishAmerica
Baltimore

First printing

Cover photograph provided by Izu Soil

ISBN: 1-4137-5964-5
PUBLISHED BY PUBLISHAMERICA, LLLP
www.publishamerica.com
Baltimore

Printed in the United States of America

Dedication
To the next generation

For my father,
the missing presence in my life

the shadow of the past is embedded in the present
tempered by the thread each moment weaves in the tapestry of
time,
memories of generations and their ancestors before them
quilted by their deeds and misdeeds.

bound with strings of love or hate,
the shadow of the past shall rise to either serenade
or haunt you,
taunt you...

Prologue

In the echo of the past
I hear weeping;
The weeping of a people scorned, burned;
Their unheard cries
In the world's conscience sleeping;

Now to live as ashes
Left to linger in their brethren's souls,
Cast in mourning cloaks
And scattered to the winds of sorrow,
Yearning for a voice, dignity and choice;

Drowning echoes of the bygone past
That has disparity and fret amassed
In the hearts and minds
Of those who, to this day, the cinders still endure,
Hoping for release at last...

this jagged present

and nothing more generous
or gainful emerged; nothing
I can call more suitably my own,
or something feathered softly
on a jagged present;

no more than a vague flickering light
through a rare glimpse that's grown
in your parents house
through the dim glimmer of your teens
when your chimera was vaulted, faulted
through its supposedly sweet scent,

and you kept squirming, arm reaching for
a savior who failed to come.
and now, a thousand thousand days ahead,
the shadows weave a tarnished tapestry,
and the light is gone…
or never came…

the former years

me: a portrait in the raw

go back to your childhood years and try to remember when
you first heard the word *shoah* and watched a tear unfurl from
your father's eyes; the word whispered like some pleated
sadness blossoming into a perfect sorrow: unsavory
across his tongue, dark as grief; an aching stab to your ear,
a poking finger at your heart, and you not even knowing why.

did not that word initiated by a demon you can only guess at,
punctuated with a sigh, always catch you by surprise? stir some
want you hadn't explicated yet? a need to understand the root,
the meaning of the frown? the despondent pronunciation loosed
into the air like a released question mark to deal with whatever
anguish
it may spring; like a free-sprung heart-cry infused with gravity
and mourning, beyond whoever prays for quick release?

what about *shoah*? a word that means holocaust; both the
cruelty
of death-pangs and the color of blood spilled at a street crossing; both
the name of a family buried long before you were born, and the
color on
a survivor's soul, ash-gray and crimson; a red and gray far
removed
from beauty, now a filler in two still-life portraits, an etch that needs to
be transported by a slew of lifetime tears; a bruise across a father's
heart, with such dark traces, one *must* venture after it—yet step

right into peril; a peril strangely firelike—so electric, it creates its own
evil glow, except that it's become a faint reticence, an immediacy that
pines for kin reduced to smoke and dust, whose name you are the bearer.

or is it just another memory transported into the portrait I've become,
regardless that it doesn't own a name? a pain that never went away from him, juxtaposed directly onto me, underlining the spectrum of a
quasi-present, defined now only by the sorrow that sustains it, birthing
the purest of blue or the grayest of gray feelings in the me of me...

when only ten years old

I became acquainted with
the past; with the tragedy of bygone ashes left to linger
as a genetic pool I was to wade in, stark and naked; a dark
swamp engulfing in black or blue whatever life would tend
to bring and bring regardless. my parents spoke of it in
Yiddish—that language of calamities—and I, not knowing
better, let it sink deep, deep into the virtue of my ID.

we dressed and looked as ordinary people, but daily had
to try appease the spirit-figures with synthetic shadows
floating between the four of us—one for every life
taken by those evil beasts in that faraway place and time;
ghostly faces in our midst carved without a trace of smile… and
one keeping score, counting out-loud every laugh we
managed… as
if it were a guilt; all of them whispering their sorrow in my ear.

and their voices got louder and louder the older I got;
chattering quietly at first, then screaming, howling, roaring
just beyond my familiar sadness… and lately, that
sadness slipped permanently into me. I rolled in it over
and over, their hurt and mine growing inside me,
spreading, spreading… and I prayed for that peace I
heard of and knew not; that joy, so absent in our home…

when I was a kid

I once helped my mother get down
the shoe box of her past,
stowed away on the top shelf of the linen closet;
a yardstick to measure the distance between then and now;
compare the rut and runnels dug around the paradigm of present,
the likes of which would cut deep into her veins
and the lewd landscape of her nonage.

she took out a stack of crinkled papers dated in the lost horizon
of that time and a pile of frayed photographs of faces and
places familiar to her, but as unfamiliar to me as the zero zeal
of soul-drought only she and papa must have known. we scanned
the memoirs long ago caught on cardboard snippets, now sepia-tinted
brittle excerpts depicting seconds of someone's prime, each with
a name only she remembered,
while she recalled dates and fates:

"this couple, was killed those years; so and so had a baby
who couldn't survive the hunger, sailed to Israel and didn't
make it—ended up in Cyprus, died of wounds that didn't even show;
this one ended up in Australia—gone
now—that one in the States—also gone by now;"
handed me each piece of the then-caught flash-points from her
shaky hands to mine, and those briefly-lived faces took on a
life again; became a
gleam in her usually sad eyes; in an instant, a new chance
to live again;

measure the flash of a split second against the ruin of time.

later she whispered quietly—more to herself than me: *"in my mind, they never left…"*

many years ago

five days into our family vacation, against an aqua
ocean backdrop, under the shade of two palm trees,
we sat upon an eiderdown of golden sand—papa, looking
very solemn, I old enough to remember war—as he unfolded
before me the atrocities from an era long ago: a cruel,
harsh demand from human demons (unbelievably, once
seemingly good citizens); his harshness behind a barbed
wire fence, the smoke and ashes all around commingled
with the pungent reek of burning flesh;

also of the family
separated from him, who on parting, gave him a big hug
and whispered the recipe for endurance in his ear: *pray every
day...for survival's sake*, and handed him the prayer shawl
he treasures to this day; and of the strangers who provided
the shield he needed... they all died there, slipped
through the cracks and black columns of smoke into the
certainty of death.

"not a day goes by,
he said, *without a prayer"*... perhaps it was a guilt; certainly
a sorrow for those he never saw again; a secret code between
them, that became also the silky strand that bound fast the two
of us by a common thread that later served to weave these
verses...

"I wish I could be him,"

he once confessed (or a much abbreviated form of it): "that father
of your dreams; that tender man who, like a dove, takes you
under his wings
and flies you over the purest thoughts, over the beauty of
unbroken lineage,
kissing you with tearless lips atop the softness of your inner velvet;

"but I have heard the death-cry of the living phantoms doomed to die;
seen those death-camp grounds running red with blood; headless
corpses and lifeless limbs bobbing on the back of wobbling carts like
ripe produce taken out to market... and the beauty of my words
dropped
past my lips—as it must when cruel intentions and genocidal
plans make
a mess of things trying to be gentle—and the phrases haven't
come since; a
silence waiting to be coined into a survival mode made sweeter by the
passing years. an invisible cage was thrown over me, which
sealed my
heart shut tight, until it vanished... or until I disappear beyond myself.

"I wish I could give you gentle plumes of words pretending to be free
streaks amidst a starlit sky, or write some form of heartrending
verse to lay at your feet... we would share parental love
between the silk

of uncorrupted memories, and float above the sunniest of fields, away from
the memory that death established. but all I can give is a bruised softness and the remnants of a broken spirit wandering the battlefield of a still maimed inner world. I can only manage the coldness of a sigh; the cry
of a barely present ghost still marching to the intensity of raised voices of interrogators in a death/work camp; only a susceptibility shielded by a
storm-cloud sweeping past the gathered sadness in my soul's decay.

"I want to give you the expression of my soul, the presence of my heart, the holy seedlings of my mind, the touch of carefree hands lingering soft
upon your fate; but my eyes still carry the sight of the dead, and my nostrils
the stench of ashes, and my ears a mound of pules and wails. I wish when
I put my arms around you, you wouldn't feel the sadness anchored to my
bones; you would only feel him, that papa you love, not allowing you to float
aimlessly on the raging river of a torrid past, which today grates my feelings
threadbare; conveying that everything is both remembering and forgetting—
which we do, and always do, regardless...

"I come to you without a song, without an easy heart, without words made
sweet by glad experience, with only a soul that weeps and weeps and weeps...

one day, I know I too will die," he kept on saying, and saying yet again, "and the children of me will miss the sin of my total absence..."

did I imagine this most rarest of retorts, or was it actually conveyed in an
absent voice that could only resonate as silence?

there was an interval of burning books

and shattered glass
and families and lives; incessant whir of terror defying any/all logic;
the rosy consequence they had always known as time, became a
cruel 1940's river they tried to cross without etching its prodigal rush
too indelibly into their minds, so they could survive. **survive?**
where? there? then? when prevailing atrocities became
a slew of sordid mists that couldn't offer any hope?

a sick, ignoble rationality was rampant in that time and place; there
was a choice of dying and one in which to wait for it. they gave
orders to kill, to plunder, to dissect lives, and the rest, without
losing any sleep over it, pointed the rifle... and the people fell
like humpty-dumptys to the drumbeat of a solid hate. and they
disappeared like some erased constants in the weightless wind.

one fell at my father's feet, lifeless eyes open and pointed to a
sunless
sky, the dark swirling darker and fading on the way down, the
wind blowing the red droplets of him upwards. it was his
best buddy. but he continued on. continued on. dead like the
intermittent dead he witnessed. dead. dead. his prayers rising
with the smoke and ashes of his kin, to an uncaring sky;

no time to stop, no time to mourn... and that was not the worst of
it; from that day on, nothing was possible, not even to walk
freely

and undisturbed, not even laughter or tears or dreaming undistrought...
not even bearing children genetically modified to cope...

they called him Lucifer...

(Lu, for short by some);
not that he had a tail and horns, not that he
straddled on the ledge of heaven, so that the
shiver he imposed would command satanic fervor—
nothing else really fit him. the seeds he implanted

in his era, black with gripe and fear, made them
think of some dark and bitter thing smeared terminal
and red and black and ash by his inner fire; egocentric
ego skirting around the tide of public opinion, shouting:
"if you want a scapegoat, I will give you one"

sadistic abomination wearing a gilded crown. evil
incarnate spinning out of control, charged up for
the kill by furthering a periphery of holocaust;
playing on the element of trust to blast a flame
against the millions, luring the damned to the killing
fields with promises of riding free upon the loop.

king of the underworld with a myriad of followers
bearing the faces of death, seeking to commit
perfect genocide. grizzly bystanders using thrill-
killing as a sport, having fun and rejoicing at
the ground-borne blood and airborne ashes;
the howling lingering long after the burning...

his name was Adolf,
they dubbed him "fuhrer,"
but the people of the Book called him Beelzebub:
master of the age of shame
bearing through eternity the burden of guilt...

once upon a time

when life was bland
and one could always live one's vow,
on safe ground to land
with faith in hand
and hope painted on one s brow,
there were those carefree youth
ready to proclaim their wit and power;

but stealthy madmen deemed it otherwise;
surrounded them with made-up lies,
shipped them off to grow less wise
than fate would have them be
if they hadn't murdered
their inborn vigor that was ripe and free,
and doomed them to a life
that wasn't theirs to gain;
living as solitary souls
condemned to suffer their own pain
in a mooted-like existence
that robbed them of a voice and choice
their present to tearfully endorse,
or forget, and try to live again;

making them into zombies
marching through the mist of time,

pushed into a dark abyss,
never to fully see, feel, be;
never to take what they were meant
to glean from the open book of life;
damned to living still—but devoid of laughter—
among the ashes left inside to smolder...
and they pry... pry... until the day they die...
and even after...

half-naked

injured, bruised and bleeding by the beating,
soaked in sweat, gasping for air, imprisoned in a barred, hermetically
sealed cattle boxcar for the week's duration of the killing-voyage,
the death-train clambered out an ominous tempo to the rhythm of
papa's pain and fright, as the mournful whistle hooted out the
tragedy of his kin's catastrophe. eight days back and forth along
the same short stretch of track without food or water, then
leaving the familiar territory of his city for the black contour of
killing camps, the pyramid of bodies piling higher every day in
the stifling proximity of crowded space—for they wanted to be free
from thirst and stench—and so they entered the fading tangibility
of the thousands of dead scurrying towards the cruel sky laid empty
of every bit of empathy.

and soon, he too lay down to sleep his final sleep… and then
his grandma's spirit came; an alighted vision interrupting his
vanilla death-dream, saying: *"wake up, it's raining, it's not your
time to die yet"*. stepping over the pyramid of outstretched arms
and legs and blanc eyes, he stretched toward the window-bars,
holding his handkerchief towards the torrential raindrops; a white
flagship of survival hanging wet and limply in the soupy swill,
then squeezed the gathered raindrops on his dried-up tongue
against death's imminent demand, gasping some solid breaths

through a tiny knothole.
a single armed station guard on the platform blew the whistle,
mocking: *"hey, Jew (mai Jidan), have a piece of cornstalk to
choke on"*, handed over speared on his gleaming bayonet; he
sucking the cud's succulence; it dripping, dripping life into his
half-
dead body; and it tided him through the entire death-ride as he
straddled the corpses of his kin, the iron dragon, tugging and
chugging
blue murder, hurrying towards a more than this turbid scene
could
possibly conceive—for it was harsh and everything he feared.
thousands perished there. only a handful survived—he among
them...or what was left of him...

survived??? **no!!!** not this; this makeshift misalignment; this
quasi-animation pretending to be lifelike!!!

on a shattered sky

that was them blown up and away,
was this expectancy, this formation of hope; gun barrel nuzzle
at their backs… and the line between is and was grew thin.

there was these children, these chosen by both man and God;
and there was this horrid scene sprung from an acoustic hate,
and it went awry, the stream they journeyed held it tight, blew it
in their laps, adorned their vanished faces. there was a them, and
there was a *"them"*… and the hate emitted began to say good-bye
to anyone that crossed the line.

that is to say, a slow way to die—some actually quite quickly;
flecked bones fallen through the flames, children sucked
in as elders reached out, drew in more than bargained-for;
and ashes fell from the sky… sparks were what they had become,
where they were, where they were going, where they'd be;
newly-sparked as living ashes less likely to remember better days…

they learned to walk amidst the weeping remnants; to stand still
and stare up at the world, praying for clemency; the me
of them a piebald shade that could never be remodified…

walking corpses proves life refuses to die…

one by one

they passed into a large cauldron of hate
that emptied in a dark river (pond of ashes, really), bobbing
in no particular order; hurried along, buried, but timeless.
hey didn't spend themselves by the hunger displayed on each
moment. something in their eyes turned away a block of
passing particles they could not remember having lived
in keeping with the hours; only to the beat of **mach shnell!!!**

they had a temporary existence within the world they
were evacuating: their past/present; a once-sweetness caged
within a vile nothingness spawned by the burdens that
nothingness
conveyed. the flight of time speeded up in the end. it got
vernacular
and a burnished ash-gray; crowded with dangers known only by
the helpless inmates, who stooped low while spending what's left
on earth in the harshness of the harshest pain.

it was just a drawn-out end, really; the trace of downcast living
lingered on. it didn't matter anyhow. in the coinciding present
of their trice, they could confuse the present with the past and
vice versa; exchange an understanding look of tiny resistance,
lean into the stillborn moment, anticipating their final night
in keeping with the law of no return…

he is hungry still—

like a tractor-trailer plowed in his
guts; and sees nothing ahead
but charred flesh and smoke
and ashes strewn in flight; a
sooty sky unwilling to
receive them;

blood and feces and vomit
stains the ground,
caked and hard,
and he wonders
how long he has,

and why the sun
got swallowed up
and everything
darkened and
stopped in its tracks.

dirt under fingernails,
on his face,
everywhere around,

belly-crawling
through the rubble,

over the frozen ground,
fingers bleeding,
lungs choked by ash...
and time draws near.

he wants to end it;
cuts his wrist
against the barbed wire,
but the bleeding stops...
it takes blood and life to die.

they opted to hold our heritage against us—

these twisted men pretending to be sane—
and made my people pass away
for the sake of theirs;
they branded them *scapegoats*
reduced to cower at their draconian measures,
shipping them off like cattle to the slaughter
to a death-filled place
where corpses were a dime-a-dozen—even
if you didn t have a dime—
where the smoke painting the unwilling sky
was a funerary black,
and beastly hounds regarded
their obscene administration
as something sacred to behold, uphold;
where a hate-created barb wired stockade
was fertile ground for criminal distortions;
where you found yourself
missing from your soul...

they say you learn from your experience

from pains begot
and lesson taught;
from bad times fraught
and battles fought;
from pathways sought
and surviving when others do not.

enduring is a good thing,
and all good things are honored,
aren't they?

but
where's the but payoff?

if holding your head up high
is rewarded with a yellow star
as a crown of thorns
that bleeds with ashes
instead of hails for being stoic and heroic;

leaving you without
a leg to stand on
to cushion destiny's tempest
which crashes waves of desolation
on the shaved heads of helpless victims…

to this day

some still don't see
how or why it all began—cruel
intentions have no valid reasons—but
they argue that pains that fester
from such bygone lamentations, should
echo only temporary rustlings that diminish
dreams and hopes of only those they touch,
leaving ashes formed in ovens
from burning flesh and bones
only upon the witnesses survived,
and cannot ever be redeemed, re-dreamed,
by the coming generations
from flames they did not kindle
or even see...

they re wrong!!! dead wrong!!! what about me???

there are people

on this planet who have never
given in to such an intangible darkness, or tasted its effects;
who believe in pain-free smiles as inbred rights
never too far away to gather up and fill their brimming cups—
vaguely reminiscent of a smooth serology
that time inevitably to only them endorses.

there are those who harbor smoky mirrors
and the allusions of a thousand myths, enough
to cloud their eyes to the black that others face,
in which can be seen the light that failed and
failed again, all the doors closed against their center,
peace of mind barely wedged into that shielded space...

these eyes are painfully blind—seeing nothing
in their darkness punching through the heavy curtain
of their bliss like a quantive motif funneled by rippling
effects of apathy, experiencing only the sweet brand of
fate that they inherited, which I imagine must exist, in
order to be tasted at all... but not for those
they cannot see...

it's all about fate—

how she owns you; the virtue
of her apathetic anatomy; ever ready to seduce you,
what gets pressed onto the legion of your hopes, letting
it get hold of the corpulent appendage that becomes
your own flesh. how you respond. the aperture it gaps,
the cleft of a mouth, a hole, the diameter of the picture it
has taken in and focused outwards.

she has this effect on you. she waits more patient
than you can ever be. sits quietly in a corner and
calculates the gravity of the matter. all of your life
she pulls and draws everything snide or vile (or bright)
together, not quite faltering, but curious what will
happen next, eager to appropriate either wings or thorns;
what she can bear, what she can wear with a
grimace, or a smile.

the verdict, when it finally comes, whispers
softly (or harsh), in your ear, or shouts it to the world,
so it can hear the blur, the death it sometimes carries, the life
it sometimes buries, the smile that never materializes, or mostly
evaporates on the familiar faces with glazed eyes,
their uncertain recovery...

this other? or another?

this me? the three of me: veil of
erosion, gulf, blueprint, plastic self,
this shadow,
this farce, over hours without end:

it *will* be interpreted as life—
not in rigor mortis, but
as an impossibility seething
with the rage of wolves;
as armed with demons, daggers,
to repel the incomprehensible;

to deter the formlessness of
the past's errancy;
applied vile ash-lash towards
bleeding lacerations,
giving it a nuance,
a past tense;

and those less-effective magnets,
these three of me:
three faceless transmutations
crumbling away,
always being pulled by my genesis,
pulleyed,

bullied,
carrying its weight in stone;

three remnants. three erosions.
three dazzling essences.
extinguished

he is gone now

but what I remember most
about my father, is his quietus—he was so
silent, sometimes I'd think he'd disappeared;
semi-present man listening for some kind
of answers from the ashes never left behind him,
that always lingered on within his strangled soul.

he hardly spoke of it, that ghastly nightmare he
endured and endured again and again after; he just drifted
quietly, aimlessly, through the sands that time provides,
as if it touched only his own fate, and had nothing to do
with ours—but it did... it did! it robbed us of

a fully-present father, like not even death could;
it erased him from our lives without a trace
of what he would have been, if only those ghastly
beasts had allowed him to survive with the angels of
his inner sanctum intact; if destiny would not have let
the ever-gnawing devils dwelling in his mind to
flourish; if it had encouraged the vile memories to
fade away and scatter in the wind of his tomorrows,
releasing his wounded soul, at least to living without
painful recollections.

but it didn't; they festered in his heart, on and on,

shredding it to bits like a Black and Decker, until it had
no choice but extricating every bit of joy in the
muted abdication that became him; the stench of cruelty
so deeply carved into his soul, it made him a fleeting
shadow fleeting though our youth without too many
words to offer or confer; without the touch of his tongue...

he said there was nothing left to say; that his words
were sacrificed upon the podium of hate; blown away
like dried-up leaves in a raging storm; like life being
sucked out by death from the pleading eyes of his family.

I fully know now; it was a deadly blow that stifled his voice,
imprisoning it in a private dungeon of unholy rest; the
river of his meager life damned and dammed and bottled up to
a
total standstill, furrowing destructive ripples through his
baffled
children's lives, not even certain what they mourned....

and his past stretched way beyond him; right into my soul,
as a never-ending string of sleepless nights...

in a troubled silence

fashioned by a grisly past
that left marks so deep,
it burned a soundless emptiness
into their being,
survivors sometimes feel like see-through
shells of what they could have been
if fate had seemed much kinder than it was.

I don t understand!!!!
why did they force their cruel angst
upon our elegant descent,
complicating an entire generation—or
even more—out of
their right to remember
only passages not weakened
by the dust that veils our imaginations
and dooms our destiny, to wither
among the thorns that ashes built?

a voice canceled

by a crooked cross and madmen
marching to Hell's wicked command,
when they buried his life in silence, the smiles and favors gone;
genocide, infanticide in crimson vile indelicately scratched,
etched in the black dust of death-camps, to this day, still
tainted black and red and vile with bile and blood,
with the smell of living futile, yet living on still,
when the night sank and the morning ended.

and his unimaginable pain crept up my arteries as well,
perhaps misshapen, or a fake, but still as real as nightmares,
calling me to mourn a lost potential, an off-center persona;
to dig deep, dig life deep underneath those horrors
that became my own, and feel how ugly it can be
when hate tears away the flesh whose name was father,
bone and soul sapped white and blue; drip-drip-dripping, one,
two, three, over and over, beneath and under;

eyes staring straight through the frozen horizon;
through unseen sky or sun or stars;
through shrouded vistas pretending to be now,
through ashes mistaken as clouds, shafting vulnerable centers
of their children left to weather life as if alone…

though still alive, he returned to us; maleric,

hysteric, half-dead, clutching slaughtered dreams, shunning even the slightest notion of a favorable future in his bloody soul; a father silenced... a childhood never fostered...

I never figured out

exactly how it happened.
I think it had something to do
with seeing so many dying all around him
in degradation and indignity,
that it stilled his need comment to convey
in an age that reaped such utter evil…

they killed his spirit and forever moored
his voice in that horrid (death)work-camp… but not
his soul. his soul wept on; lost in the color black
and buried in a permanent tomb of wounds
that festered like putrid raw sewage
for the rest of his deadened days,
darting invisible jabs in his heart
that extended even to the living,
gouging scars further than
only his own generation…

papa's frequent stony silences

were frayed threads we were made to weave through
our fragility; a common link we shared intuitively against
what could be worse: an overwhelming need to cry, shout, rant;
call out names of those we never knew—as he sometimes
did when even silence wasn't enough—the drenching
nightmares
mamma had to deal with almost nightly, sometimes night after night,

the wails: *I can see it,* he'd whimper, *doesn't let me sleep: when
I returned and found the body of my sister Hanna's infant,
bullet-riddled, nothing more than bits of flesh and blood
splattered all around, next to the carnage of her six-year-old
brother Nathan and their mother's, even in death, still reaching
for them... she was only ten months old, for god's sake...
how could they? why? why? ...;*

and sis and I shivering in the next room, even in the hottest nights;
times we listened to the commotion of those nightmares, dreams
of another time; full of plagues and torture; full of names we'd gotten
to know; and mama rocking him in her arms, singing him back
to sleep...
after, he remembered only fragments of his dreams: a human
slaughterhouse, a weary line of figures marching near a frozen lake,
a mother holding tight an almost living infant, shot through her child;
barracks fetid, alive with lice and stink from excrement and

decaying humanity...
those were the times we longed for the frequency of his silence,
the peace it seemingly conceived within his soul. we welcomed
them, those silences; embraced them like an old friend;
someone we
had always known, a something to be cherished... I think it was the
price he paid for surviving when others didn't... and it became us...

I learned early on: everything inside can die, but not your soul;
it just lies in wait for you to even try forget, and then it bleeds
into a silence, and if you let it bleed its sorrow, it will let
you live and survive in that silence... but it also swallows
everyone else in its proximity...

in the frequency of his silences

he once told me he remembered other times he used to call
his youth, so long ago, his kinsmen, moored deep within their
ancient heritage, hadn't even dreamed of ashy endings yet;
cinders
hadn't risen; ashes failed to fill the sky—too busy painting
clouds
with silver linings, let alone a shroud of man-prone soot—
ash was something stove pipes made in winter;

there was no name yet for what arose out of evil men's
intentions,
or what turned the trembling earth ashen, or crimson; no word
yet
for the stench of burning human flesh; why they died, why
their smoke darkened the tormented sky,
and for the atrocious conduct men without mercy could devise;

if they'd known a term as holocaust, they would have never
stayed in that country of blame; ancient towns and shtetls,
where civilization wasn't found yet and time refused to leave
or be a guidepost to the future; where stars shone brightly in the
midnight sky, and ear-locked children seldom watched them
streak downward to their own doom;

no one had yet seen their own blood, or that of another;
nor felt the sting of cruelty and shame; their feathered dreams

took them only to a deep longing for nothing changed...just for the limned Savannah promised in their sacred Torah...

a belated piece of voice

the words he had for a lifetime harbored, were papa's constant
silent companions; they stayed cowering too long as a bleeding
emboli which festered in the half-light of his being, separating
him from living even half-full. I sensed them, felt them trying
to claw their way out sometimes, but they were not allowed to
puncture the solid wall they built, by his impotent tongue... but
on that day, 30 days and a billion tears after his passing, as mama
and I went through his yellowed papers in that dented, old metal
lunch box he had hidden in the back of his closet; *there it was!!!*
in his own handwriting: a too-few page unburdening of what he
could never ever outright utter, entrusted to the silence of a scant
few distant pages; a series of jolts set to neutral recto-sheets, every
word an etched pain, a sculpted sorrow; multi-layers of phrases
in broken English rubbing against each other like grating sandpaper,
sent as a belated piece of voice... wailing, screaming, of his
work/death-camp trial...

it is in that silent paper-distance, so vastly separated from his
muted presence, that I truly found him...

and now, many years and tears and scars later, mama too is earth
to earth, ashes to ashes. her almost nightly visitations convey they
are together once again... at last at rest... at rest...

but what of me???? what of me????

God promised

sun after rain;
rainbows arching across
a soggy terrain, but not in one
left ruined in the old dynasty of
burning flesh, or drowning
in the prelude of blood-rich rivers.

certainly not so in the life of a survivor's child
lost in the folds of her ash-damaged image...

I think of how pain rhymes with rain;
how fate with hate;
and how sharp a stab
such a verse would be
if only I could
get it past my pen...

and still it refuses to come...

it's not certain

what kind of phrases,
or promises you could try to make
that would mean anything at all
to a squandered being,
who due to a childhood wasted
on the podium of a cremated past,
did not learn the art of truly living,
leaving it with nothing to appease its soul.

you could say you're sorry, try to make
it up by placing her in joy's way, but it wouldn't mean
a thing coming from an empty heart
lacking life and every-which-way shooting silence
as a means to your salvation,
holding ingrained flaws not of your making,
and trying to fix irreparable things with just
your childish wits about you.

you could even try release its wings
from the chains you wrapped around them...
but in vain... its fate is sealed by those very chains.
or you could say to yourself: deal with it later;
another time... next year... hoping it would go away,
disappear when you've discovered that you haven't... but
it never does... never will... just festers as a bequeathed
silence you've inherited by way of paternal descent...

a blast of voices

there was always a range of voices roaring out a roar—a blast from
the past of sorts. there was always some dark, some haze, smudging
the imprint of this sinister paraphrase of mine; a little gritty, a little flinty;
to be swallowed whole and spittled out again as an array of flop, messy glop
and sop; blurry menace reflected on the mirror of this sick, slick scenario, and a slew of harsh effects deflected off the harsher version it
incurs: a contorted barrier

that draws and draws this onlooker into an off-ballance, left wondering
what to do next with the compliance: press a finger against the shutter of
a still-life camera, or point a gun to the nearest person: yourself, finger
ready to pull; or with sudden change of mind, point at anyone in
sight, saying: it's your fault nothing survived... and shoot

now that I have children of my own;

now that I scan laundry lines with flapping linen
strung like white flags in the hopeful wind,
polish silver, save nickels for a rainy day, arch my
back so I can see a bit of blue in my sky; I still don't
know what I am: a parasol-mother trying to protect my
kids from every storm, every deluge they encounter,
a chocolate-chip-cookie-mom trying to hand them every
sweetness possible; or a stunted woman, an empty voice,
a lingered bruise, my persona gnarled and bumpy, my
soul black as my charred heart?

now that life has woven a promise around my soul, made
as if an old friend at last reunited for a brief moment—like
a prayer answered, I still usher in the night with hidden
beasties lurking in the dark; still breathe the sweat of
something in me, longing, longing, longing; pining for
something else... more, more than I have been given; more
than this once-in-a-lifetime love and the children from that
love; more than I have taken from the past... much more than
that something in me that somehow rejects these holy gifts
and collapses me inward, while I stand by... helpless...

how can I ever forget?

I try, but the past won't have it;
it wants to have its say;
my father's memories control my life;
I've tried to hide them deep, deep;
but if I do, it's worse;
they seem to gnaw my soul to bits
until I have no way to keep it
glued together, so I resort
to shooting words on empty pages
with an ink-pen bleeding tears instead of ink,
in the hope of quenching flaming fires
that deposited a heap of ashes
in my heart; with every beat,
dispersing sooty chunks into the way
I think and feel and breathe...
and write...

haunted, taunted

everything; every celebration, every
misfortune is clouded by the prevailing mist
of my parents' tragic history—and more added daily;
to every verse created,
to every smile portrayed without permission.

for once, could not the shadows of the past
not haunt me? taunt me? daunt me?

could not the phantoms find a different venue
for their thirst to still adhere, to gulp,
and gulp, and gulp, regardless,
the forum of my nights, the litany of my days?

pain changes everything...

over fifty years

these misshapen horizons have enveloped
around themselves; around me, when I was
too young to know it would engulf me if I let them...

and I too became ashes on the shoulders of
survivor-parents; held hostage on vagabond time,
in the midst of those who grieved something I couldn't
even fathom; for faces grown not too dim in the minds
and hearts of the survivors.

those long-ago contortions live still, their unforgettable
history is still there, surviving inside me: the huge
implosion in the me of me when I try to piece myself
together; try to shed the skin of my ancestors, who stand
there, cardboard suitcases in hand bulging to the brim
with skeletons and generations of sorrow and angst...

ash settles on everything in sight...

this annulling faction

this living with the past—not even
your own—feeds on itself,
churning, wresting,
dangling like
a nest of vipers.

the knot noosed around my neck
tightens like a choke,
twisting voices from the deep
time-chiseled into a contortion;

no way out
of its wish to strangle,
mangle my legacy of singularity,
as I lie six feet under
its shadow.

I always sensed there was a door inside

opening the way to sunshine.
that door was always locked, the shape
of distance metered by the space it shielded
always closed off
like an archaic shrine
protected from this living day,
that always filtered in the dark
scattered on the walls, pieced
together by the pain it hoarded.
sometimes I thought
we'd find the key; the
heat of our pulsing heartbeats beating
down the door,
shattering the rusty locks,
and the relief of fresh air,
the swirling possibility
of filling the vacancy with life.
a closed room and heart
is like winter
with frost blanketing
everything that could live
into a sort of living death;
cold-blasted by a gust of wind
snaking up the spine.
I fell asleep in front of that door;
frozen years ago into an iceberg
of my own…

leave far behind the spider web of bitter words

that triggered you so far. you'll have to learn to find other
ways of writing the poem. it will no longer carry you to the
other side of the shore, where origins begin to weigh heavy
and night appears to near.

their seeds were planted during childhood, when your mother
nursed you at her breast; genetic seeds planted by the Nazis,
who tried to scour the world of a generation of innocent souls,
for simply being rooted in the tradition of a single God Who
declared these chosen seeds to become as multifarious as stars.

the scant survivors crossed the border to this side of the world,
where the darkness ever filtered to the surface, to build a
chamber
full of ashes for their offspring, who tried to write the poem
as a means of surviving the disturbance. but clearance was
not there, you discovered; its images had changed; could not
be reconstituted in a different landscape;

the focus was far enough to be lost in the horizon of the free,
and where it remains hiding in its usual place, under your vain
attempts to write the tragedy of total sobs… a rarity of penitent
words exhaled on a daily basis…

you find you can't escape the savage murmur of fire when corpses
sizzle out their last and meager breath within your dream-world;
can't learn to stop connecting the past with the present poem;

for it haunts you, daunts you, waiting eagerly for you to sacrifice a slew of tears...

I've been mouthing my tick and trundle words

to the sky incessantly, but still there is a question
mark that hangs, reluctant to observe the magnificent
oneness they confer. roars are bouncing off the rooftops,
and eardrums are scanning the world for the refuge of a
liberated song, immortal in its sanctified glissando.

you've heard the old adage: reading is a spectator sport,
and not everyone one can see what's hidden in the text.
meanings are in no hurry to escape your gaze, a slew of
sorrow buzzes out a sentence to your eyes. it knows a
hundred hungry words for "existing" for "living" but it
remains still and slick in your archaic throat.

there are committees set up to figure out our problems and
why the fault-line is as static as a rocky mountain... in vain;
sometimes I think I see the wind of change going about
its work, the air under its bull's-eye arrow wishing to be
liberated from the past's dust, the clouds over a bald eagle
seeking to clear away the human-spun debris; and I ask:

who am I in that story? a woman watching the fine line
blurring between calm and terror? between good and evil?
the sinners fingering Rosaries in the shadow of churches,
the dying flickers reminiscent of some long-ago light by
now extinguished; not a lit window in sight, not a candle
to luminate a traveler's path...?

from the spindled trademark

of this liquid now, this catalyst for
marbleized sunlight surviving on the fringes
of a soul's horizon, comes a sordid pulse
stopped only by an appropriate condition.
a sweetness forbidden to our senses
arrests our corrupted innocence,
proclaiming an awakened magnitude
upon the collective black mass that has become
our modified chimera.

but the red tongue of someone else's memories
snaps loose, dedicated not to us; only
to the wetlands of that soul, that quagmire of gray
cygnets; awkward puddles birthing spikes,
and menacing parcels of interspersing broodings
between the silk-grass of the now and the thistle
of yesterday, too sure-footed to disappear...

another sleepless night

sad with incurable wounds… known to me
like someone else's sickness,
I lie listening to night as a series
of discomfited assessments
seeking to be quashed
by sleep, to leave a black gouge
in the gape of day, the scream of silence
loud and clear. but some
shadow found its way past my eyes,
gargantuan and looming…

another sleepless night,
staying wide awake, looking
straight ahead and intolerably vulnerable.
the one candle by my right,
still flickers on for hours, throttling
flares in an excess of light, looking much
like a phantom-finger on the wall.

and still, sleep is wasted on me,
except for a gathering of misbegotten thoughts
piled high against the shudder.
sometimes the thick ticking of the clock
plays its secret games—and one of them
is how to keep me from the sandman;
and the rain too, joins the conspiracy,
drumming on the rooftop with fierce reverberation,

the small and uncomfortable brush of branch
tapping at the window, a well-bred
countdown to approaching dawn.

someday this most-consistent torment
will pass, or at least dwindle to a faint pang, and
I will sleep with the sorrow of what
I will keep and cannot have...
but later... much later, I assume...

a fissure of macho cringes

I'm just a scavenger lost in the frown-field
of our stone-cold home, where
love floats belly-up,
with roots disentangled from the sea of
dislocated dreams.

I lie awake again, trying to compute the fissure
that replaced what could be joyous with the glum,
with sheer abdication of a life well-lived;
lips clenched so tight
they resemble macho cringes.

what laughter there was,
lies buried deep into the rutted soil,
eclipsing the fantastic legend of the great
impostor: life; while I, like a choking vagueness,
continue extending *apologies and guilts*;

by now bruised and dented, trying to dodge
a bucketful of dripping tears and a myriad
of angry vowels and articulations
messing with my pen....

a search... a search...

a being always wants more. measure the indecision:
the bitterness of the past or a present's sweetness. how
much better the consequence of both: first the
galling then the savory. I have evaded sleep far into the

night with the same results: first you need the bitter then
the semisweet, at least. a soul needs both: the harsh and
chafing/the mellow succor. words shine where silence gapes
like missing notes of a half-forgotten poem. you won't

believe it when I tell you that to make waves you must
splash; to enter turbid waters and rotate your oars.
take the language of symmetry and swirl the hulk of its
asymmetries. sing a lullaby every human heard and
make it sound like thunder;
then continue searching... searching... searching...

listening to tongues of flames lodged deep within you,
their crackled web snapping, sapping, gasping fierce
and reaching out to ravage anything in sight and what they
mean by searing; about us, altogether not here, engulfed by
the past, is like resting on your laurels; the terse gasp gives
off an acrid waft.
and you must go and do your own search for closure...

but the soul is neutral. only the mind knows what it
hatches can be harsh or sweet, chafing or emollient to a heart

that listens to the lap of world-squalls: piles of sweetnesses or scorns against the heart. a kind of sharing among familial members shooting either silences or arrows towards their sacred spaces...

beyond the evils of midnight

on the cusp of queasy sleep; back to the wintry years,
behind the spiny gossamer of guilt and created gutterfloods
and crenelated doors, you find a smudge worthy of
recording, spun at the slow speed of 3 a.m.; a thin glitter
trying to save you, help you survive the wounds; where
so long ago a contusion put down roots too deep to be
uprooted... not even with the tremor of this fickle pen, that would
put down, and yet again, anything abbreviated by your hand.

bloodshot eyes with a halfway slit, migraine drilling in a
sworn crater of your skull, you write about the alibis of
guilt and shame and something you cannot even name;
one short stop to the frontier locked in the rattle of yourself,
already shaped as a crazed and bloody scream...

the burden of ash

harmony, I long for you, your blank, your slow-white scar; you,
in all your amity and astral pompatus, your coy unopened lips
wiped free of stormy petrel always set in a solitary smile;
caesura thirsting for some piece of peace; unrest interrupted
by a placid space; you, driving all the caws away; spilling over
the low lights, your wind chimes always ready to be indulged;
that necessity for completing the circle of your urge, the design
and pattern around your splendor committing you to calming
cycles we so easily forgot. forgot.

you, so gentle and tender, caressing against a purple need, and
me reaching out for your pool of quiet with long thin fingers
pulling at your celebration, a fragment of light caught in your
particular dawn, in the glitter of a sunset, into a distant moon,
and you always exchanging such a sweet embrace with me,
the feathers of my own need floating gently in your yellow sky,

smooth and calm as windshear will allow, the greenery uncurled
beneath me welcomed with a sudden summer breeze, and me
slow-walking in your balmy sweetness, the orange bells of lilies
ringing softly in the calmness of a rainfall, the beat of raindrops
heard for miles ahead; for your rare soft touch on me, your
swanlike silence a soft hum floating on the river time like a sleeping
moment; that place I've always been arriving at, only to

discover the sameness of a passing darkness—when it

swallows every bit of flesh there's nothing to be found there
but the dark of nothingness—you, always replaced by a ghost,
a tumult, a sorrow, the odd-sounding droom of a war I did not
know, the first call of gunshot breaking the glissando stillness
into pieces, the silence of an ash-infested brood not born of

my own singularity, but of another...

such a heavy shadow to carry. oh the weight of it...

resolution

there's no way out but going there! the desire to see, to be
in that world of ashes
as a wildness trying to appease the inner devil
with some short-lived satisfaction,
the last dying ember endless in its passing;
with one foot in the grave
the other on a slimy peel, for me, it
is at least a harsh necessity.

and then my resolution:

I'm face to face
with dust.
if I don't go, I will inherit it even in the earth,
where I will gather it most,
sour it with something of myself
that is eternal for eternity; if I don't go,

I will collide with earth;
the pressure of being a curse
indented in the near and far of me;
that of me scattered to sky;
in that deep that doesn't die…

my head is spinning out of control

my heart is shattered, battered;
my soul has lost its purpose;
my appetite has vanished;
my bones, my flesh, demand account.
I'm slipping fast away from my reality;
only sleepless nights
and dreamless days prevail.

there's a harsh truth to face:
I cannot reconcile the flames my people
suffered then, with what the truth endorses
now. I must visit Hell's horizon for myself,
to find the stranded phantoms of my kinsmen's
souls, left to linger all alone amongst the
scattered ashes left behind by those
pretending to survive...

I can't return to dust before I see
the unmarked graves of vanished corpses
crying out to be remembered; snuffed-out
cinders left to smolder in a cursed
bloodstained ground, devoid of just remorse.
I must seek justification—
for a new lease on life.....

the search for closure

the journey has begun!!!

looking out the hotel window, it seems the night had
done what's easiest: scattered a feather eiderdown of
black across this nonjudgmental sky, so I cannot even try
discern what's hidden, waiting for me in the dark beyond.

dawn hasn't even stirred, but a backyard watchdog rouses
long enough to throw a bark towards some nondescripted
shade, which, by now, has taken over everything,
like a haunting phantom seeking verification.

phantoms wait to be awakened. ghosts wait to be endorsed
by light; ghosts that have folded themselves into balls of
invisibility, waiting for some bit of human stirring to wake
them and claim them as their own... what fools we are!... not
knowing ghosts are never to be had or owned...

I, too, wait impatiently for dawn, to start my long-awaited
journey into that dark interval of soul-bitters accrued through
a
lifetime of secrets and silences...but I'm so far withdrawn
into the dark before me, my thoughts do not endorse me.
I wonder how the mirror of tomorrow will portray me: invisible?
or resurrected? still bruised? or swept free of the myopic
nightmares I have lived and lived regardless...?

what passes me by in the taxi

is brewing full of counterclockwise swishing vistas to the eye;
the light not yet successful to array what is written on this day:
this fateful day I'm to embark. what passes are safe harbors for
the fortunates sleeping still inside; miles of fairytale farmhouses
and red barns on the not yet lighted hillsides, almost-yellow rape
fields not fully eradicated by the half-light, the winding country road
where others have gone before me. across are clumps of wooded
patches with a dark perplexity inside; here a whitewashed cottage,
there an open vista and a steeple spire almost visible in the distance.

a highly-hued clarity of flashes of a childhood never fostered, deep
remnants of a glacial girlhood in a stunted home, also pass by;
whole parcels of time in yesterday's furrows, interspersed with the
autumn-tired meadows flashing by; flashes more real than even
the earth can know: what's consequential to the real, what's passing
by, inside and out; bushel-fulls of fallen disarray upon the hazy
counterpane of the cumulus of both mind and windowpane.

almost there… to enter the silent sentry; witness of that long-ago
time to rising ashes, still alive, I'm certain; still hankering, I know,
to be vindicated by the trekking multitudes…

I'm here at last

in this cursed quasi-graveyard,
seeking silhouettes of at least some approximated
answers, or an explanation that will lay my soul to rest...

more than fifty years have past since the almost-whole
of a generation perished from undigested hate and
failed compassion, saying nothing until they had
succumbed; cut off from the wheel of life by
monsters wearing twisted crosses on their armbands, who
riffled through those starving shadows as if it had nothing to
do with them as being human...

more than fifty years... and death still lingers
in the muted silence; the tears and sweat and blood of
the lost seeped deep into this hateful clay... but the
glaring sign above the entrance still hangs stoic, heroic-like,
declaring the deceitful words: **arbeit macht frei** (work
makes free)—words that ended dreams and hopes of millions
of vanished figures— placed conspicuously, so new
arrivals will see and dare believe their empty promise...

deep in thought

I wander through the defiant portals.
I take my first step, and sink deep into the past,
the gap between then and now disappearing
like a fleeting shadow that never hoped to triumph; only
to bring me closer to this moment,
so I may try unearth some fitting explanations, which
I cannot seem to see here anywhere I look;

each step takes me further and further from the
present, until everything I have finally begun to be,
becomes one with a history that cannot justify
not even one tomorrow, until the last step is
taken—that is, if these blasted ashes I cannot
dislodge from my tortured mind still remain
in my today's concerns...

another step, and I'll be lost forever in the
never-never-land of oblivion's dark recourse
of nothingness...

this is real!!!

this is what I inherited!!! everything
moves slowly here; so slow, it seems frozen to the past.
I can see the orphaned tears and fears and reams of
doom and death streaming out through the gate behind me.
it makes me dizzy how they move through me and leave
a gnawing hurt, innavigable, portent, hard to appease; and
then it opens up old wounds again.

I am here because I need this place. need to look for the
answers that it so far sorely fails to render; as proof that I can
harbor something to be hated and abhorred, and still appease
the demons with sotto offerings, to move forward; on
from ingrained traces of a death I didn t brush; from
suffering, suffering, like pellitory thorns inside.

I am going to stare it down; braid with it, gray and stark as
tangled pain in walls and stacks and rusted barbed fences.
I need to be shocked by its frank quietness; mauled by its
blunt silence—that total scream of silence; the thought of it,
the feelings it evokes, the inner rawness it provokes.

I need to wake up somewhere else and know I am
there and not stuck in a past I didn t even suffer.
I need a resolution to slip into me; missing link,
fervor, mammoth lust for life... so absent, it's eroding;
the world as it could be: white for once, not filled with black,
with looming clouds. not so dangerous, so painful...

with a stripped bravado

day barely cracking into a reluctant
dawn, I trip forward without apology or penitence, a spectral
blood-trail dripping behind like a fluidity slithering across
the fierce terrain. the night of stolen winks, which always
weaves a quintessential dread of what isn't anecdotal, sighs
a promise of sweet release; but it goes remiss, like the
night, who is capable of leaving with the morning light,
slipping into the distance like an aqueous shadow.

oh, how the cold winds blow through my dormant soul, all
along my
trembling body, its temperature a neutral compass of my
trepidation;
how prearranged ahead of time the semi-orbit sway of dread,
pressing its murkiness against my hereness, the somnolent
shadows calling me by name, in hinged notes of quirky
rubrics…

in awkward strides, I stretch to catch a glimpse (if only
temporarily) at
the star-less darkness trying to survive, silhouetted barely with a
round girth of moon, with which the chill will merge, but all
I see is an almost-black currency etched across a fearful sky
straining to
survive, like a fading star struggling at the jurisdiction of the sun.

feverishly, the smell of bloody history and wet dust everywhere,
I scream inwardly the stifled scream I carried there since birth,
loud and bloodcurdling as a total scream can be, the stillborn bellow
lying heavy with my heart; in one clenched hand the holy book,

a thing
held sacred by my people, and in the other, my constant
companion: this,
my faithful, eagerly-awaiting notebook, which will see me
through the trial;

and both ground and paper tundra is ready to receive the stone-cold
little nuance of my spirit. then silence... and all the ghosts have
risen up to greet me.

I've been here

a thousand times... but haven't. every minute
ticks by slowly, is brushed aside by the gloom pending.

step by step I move forward, unaware to do so,
until I have achieved my end, this inner doom to fend;

I am here to pen an amnesty of the burnt-in past-torn vista,
where ghosts lurk behind every timeworn edifice, between

collapsed hopes and dreams buried under yesterday's
apocalypse, executed in killing pits by eager killing squads;

mass murder and unprecedented war crimes... brutality
taken to perverse extremes, and millions slaughtered—not

just here, but at Babiyar, Dachau, Bergenbelsen,
Buchenwald, Aushwits, Birkenaw, Treblinka, Maydanek...

I am here to come to grips with the past; try quash the hidden
flame that feeds it to the next, when it will burn again...

it is a forceful place

this inappropriate avenue, where the carnal black
of inhumaneness hangs over the totality like a curse,
so vivid and sharp, it pierces the eye of the beholder, dimming
the glowing hope of finding some resolve hidden

behind it.
what used to be a mass of humans is gone now, and the remains
lie dry and lifeless, silent as a stone. stone cold. stone dead;
its nonplus vitriol tumbling in the wind like flapping sheets
hanging on a laundry line; a sag of blank expanse ready for an
altered view: the filtered old trying to circumvent itself into
some other
fabrication.

the ultimate nobility of things was washed out, replaced by ash, and
allowed to mingle in the gutter with the sludge in the unforgiving
hold of the unsuspecting cumulus; and who would step forward
to denounce it?
is it some human flaw, that the reigning vileness reinvents itself each
decade in the cold light of change? some of it in the midst of what
was then and there, and some out there where everyone ignores it?
then bursts into flame and swallows every other

version of itself
and turns it into another fiend… only this time, it silently
claws deeper into the darkening sky, dissolving into the fragility
of nations; unafraid of being felled, always a figure which
remains untouched, but catastrophic… swirling in its

own black orbit.

beneath the cold dark of not-yet dawn

a silence that engulfs you,
the unbearable now fading stars of a silent sky
doing nothing but hanging there, quietly,
trying to disappear into the lacquered space
between the universe and you;

like the ghosts of some vicious past,
everything is stilled by their August
retreat into the scowl of history...
they must have a reason for it;

to install the peace of night upon this
dreadful place; a peace that dies a
thousand deaths each morning;
a peace that never exists for those
entombed within the ground it suffers;

those fading into the darkness
of its power,
where they can't survive
in the moment of that silence...

thousands died here

on this cursed piece of heartless earth; a Jew every
45 minutes turned to smoke—the SS boasted of it—45 minutes
train to chamber/train to cinders; 12,000 a day, hundreds of
thousands, millions in all, from whips to ashes... no one left
alive here. later only empty trains departed... everyone
knew, the world knew, and no one cared... no one cares now;

thousands died here, as they bled and burned and yearned for
mercy; blood mopped up with scarlet-tarnished shovels
scooping globs of clots into the fresh-dug hollows by tainted
spades that witnessed raw flesh oozing rusty-crimson on
aborted grounds; voiceless shadows straddling on the pulse of
hate; rows of names on endless lists; the wasted with numbers
etched on wasting arms; starved, raped, bullet-riddled to the wall;
cursed, fused, used, abused, till sweat and tears and blood
beaded on their see-through cheeks;

hunched over, squatting low or leaning into barbed wire,
fire-charged current seeking flesh to sear, they prayed; asked
their ancient God what to do;
what it was that they had done—in the same voice
they used to praise Him;

but the total silence screamed back a hollowness; a
response of broken vows; all they heard was
a range of vacant echoes; all they saw was blackened
pigment on a bright-red earth, and bones melted into ash;

and they took their place in line...

promises

of 'liberty through work' dissolved into a
density of thick atrocities, when they plodded on
between head-high banks of snow, goaded on by
screaming guards; demons armed with bayonets and
fists and pistols, the quivering threat of fire hovering
over the doomed queue of humanity, pushing aside
everything they held dear, as they hardened into a
transmutation of their former selves, leaving on their
hearts a thorny stronghold where permanent jagged
stones were born.

they wanted to survive, fly away to the sunshine,
away from the ash and stench, from tattooed numbers,
from the slow, rough torture. but they were mired in
their own blood-mire, remembering only all the
elementals of their past—not their arrival here, where
they were made to cower, whimper, die.

if we are beaten, they thought, *somewhere, someone*
will remember in the nocturnal density of the future,
the black of our soot, the graveyard of our blood; will
shout against the same sky without a shot in response.

but all they could do, is prepare for a cruel sky, a slow-
pleated death... or something too quick.

I know... my father told me so...
in his choice of paper voice...

when they arrived on this scene

it seemed benign enough—if not cheerful,
congenial at least; a pleasant quartet of inmates
playing softly, and other trappings to entice the weary into
thinking all is well and fun and games;
but this place was not what it seemed!!! **they burned people
here!!!**—but first they sucked out all the sweetness from a life
already frail, by promoting vicious acts towards its invalid apex;

it was a baleful of lies and false pretense that could carry no
defense; a place of broken families and interrupted dreams,
where trust was abandoned to the past, hopes scattered
in the wind, and dignity was turned to dust;

a place where charlatans on power trips messed with
helpless heads and hearts and souls, turning memories to
fantasies that never were; where swaddled frostbitten feet tread
the crimson ground littered with living corpses ignored right
out of existence by demons posing as men; where
children were split apart before their parents eyes, and
so-called doctors corrupted the womanhood of many, leaving
them forever missing children, to a great extent mourning
absent motherhoods and fighting a raging storm of hate
that mercy won't admit;

an ashen site of the living dead and the dead trying to survive;
where smiles were replaced by persistent frowns and
blanked-out stares; where life became impossible to bear,
and wrongful separation from the living—from living—
offered only fear and the invalid verdict of being
both invisible and abandoned…

they were beside themselves

didn't like this place at all.
it was chipping away at their morale, now deeply troubled
by sleep-deprivation and soul-mutilation,... *they were at
the mercy of NAZI commands, for goodness sake!!!*

exiled, broken inside, reeling at the evil confrontations
that split their dreams apart, they valiantly plodded on,
sheets of sweat and tears washing over numbed cheeks
glinted like disabled diamonds, and dried-up blood
trickling on the absent faces supported visions of despair;

their reverence for life constipated by the ghastly atrocities
encountered, their sanity was waning fast. facing at last
the reality of their mortality, they felt the weeping ghosts
of a thousand phantoms that once endured the same reward
roaming the haunted barracks where death awaited
impatiently to have its way.

most succumbed, but some still survived—my father among
them—insisting that victory lies in the mind, in the heart,
in the soul. the thought of feeling normal again someday
was all that saved them from death's (and man's(?)) cruel
grasp...

mostly it was quiet...

deathly still, in that godforsaken
killing field—except for the Gestapo barking out commands;
but they knew they were at war—not with a living enemy,
but in a battle of their own senses, between the will to live
and the need to die; discharged from still writhing in the
gripping meshes of a strangling net;

from enduring long treks on frostbitten feet, wind-swept
rain cutting at their absent flesh, bearing screams from the
dying slammed alive in snow-filled ditches, which in the
spring boasted of their cache of corpses bent in all the
wrong places, by then hardened into twisted configurations,
showing the hard impact on their wasted souls as death by
suffocation laid its toll; all life extinguished, whether
dead or not...

of course, even glancing left or right was strictly *ferbotten* ,
at the risk of dying faster than they already were... and so
they plodded on, just as dead as those released from life...

what they carried within

was as precious as what was taken away;
it bound them more tightly to their faith than
the vast cruelty that spearheaded them
away from their loved ones; it would attest to the
heritage, it would try explain how the intangibles
of a nation could hold and further evil, death;

some rebelled—too few to mention. the rest,
sensing death could not be swayed from the realm
of lacking hearts, remained wrapped in quietness:
the darkness of despair; those surviving the
burning, the ashes, never getting past the dying,
grieving always, enduring ever the silence left by
the millions floating upwards with the smoke;

untold generations murdered, wrenched from the land;
the same blood coursing through the vanquished and
survivors; both inscribed as lost souls, forged below
earth, pressured in darkness. those catapulted above,
as twinkling stars raying down a sea of black diamonds…

what is this place?

they thought; "this *Gehenna* built by earthly demons;
this is what I must resign to? to life wind-tossed
to despair? to concessions given up for nothing? to
a fate disfigured beyond recognition? not kissed by
gold-trimmed decency or silver kindness, or silky dreams
and sanguine hopes of help to come? not blessed
by laughter, or love even in disguise as humane treatment?"

by basic human needs at least pretending to be,
if not comforts, at least bearable, or work that makes one
feel of worth? to hope, in vain trying to gain permission to
emerge; damned to wrongful endings that don't even presume
to be happily-ever-afters?

and how they prayed: "*God, give me back my life
or take it swiftly*" ... it also was my father's prayer;
he once told me so...

after all

of those evil men's mistakes crashed to earth,
earth shattered with the fury of their impact,
casting an unholy flicker across this landscape,
leaving bones and flesh in compromising positions,
a resembled silence falls over the fragments
posited as a range of rusticating cinder-layers; a litany of ghosts
spent in the total feel of absence; factitious, frangible,
having guardianship over this bellicose patina.

I can feel that silence; that aphorism on either
side of midnight, when there's nothing left but stars sending
pulsing ribbons of galvanic light across the shamed heavens.
will the broken balance be a mere syntax of a bygone scream,
or will it dissipate into the solidarity of this dark singularity,
once again
to breathe the desecrated breath of measured mass-
humanity striving to become a thing remembered; a resistance
to
the weight of guilt; the verity of wind shaping
the great divide into a compendium of axioms....
or nothing?

it is a cool day in autumn

the earth lying underfoot
like a sealed hieroglyph
waiting to be given premise.

how quietly the emptiness
moves between the barracks;
a fluidity like mist sifting
through the need of morning;

one that could easily blend
into one continuous regret
fully detailed into notice,
scarcely kept from objurgation;
the souls discarded, wasted,
handing out a sorrow...

the sun has almost risen now

from the hold of night's horizon,
and all the shadows have receded;
have turned into an unending stretch of clouded haze.
there seems to be no room for me in this shadowless world.
I have thrived on phantoms, and nave not allowed the defeated
shadows of the past to return to what they must: dust… dust…

soon I will make it to the ovens, smoky twinges staining
my accrued day into the harshest field of sorrows. I am a woman
without dreams, even the poignant is pointless; spread
thin and faint. quiescent vanity turned into a brutal concept
of a dim autobiography. gone from pot… to rust… to dust;
a particular rustle knocking my reach away from being counted.

I've made it to this place, and the sky hangs gray in front of me;
a span that's turned the voices it hides hollow, and I'm too blue
to decide if the inner ghost is my claim to life, or if the reverse
is to be echoed through the gray around me. all around me.
all around me is a deep crevice—aside from the chasm of this place—
a dark horizon with no need for me. how could my life have
become so inanimate, so picked clean of flowers and dreams?

with plated facelessness

the eyes of the beast hover, so
precision-glinty in their cruel mask, they might be sparks of
evil in a dark-like sky. its stars in a blind cosmos residing in its
own benign axiom of shadow close-ups, raises its solid mass,
its universal four-cornered spread across the earthly
hemisphere,

its claws quickening against this gray horizon, parts the world of
balance, unbalancing it until it is as heavy as heavy
forethought,
silent as the absence of first accusations... or last, like an unstable
alchemist in a galaxy of raw expanse keeping quiet in the face of
inadmissible recollections...

and a grievance dangles high in the barely day-lit cumulus, ready
to engulf the survivor and the dead: the total fragility of this day,
black mucus in a clump of clay mingling with the mass of gray
skulls. and later, renamed *living* , they walk randomly into the
aftermath the beasts created, startling stark with darkish fumes
covering the ground,

carefully altered from the iridescent intricacy that once displayed
across the pattern of its former form... breathing in and out... in
and out...a slew of human wounds and lesions, puss-pink and moist
and seeping out as someone else's sorrow, dry and lifeless as death...

a tooth for a tooth (gold or otherwise)

is ancient justice (according to the Book)
but eyes and teeth and souls from millions
who secrete themselves muted?!!!

but why these innocents?
why snuff out millions of genetic candles?
snip off bits and pieces of themselves,
admitting them to a convoy of the doomed?

what victory triumphs from gouging
eyes of chocolate-eyed children
exterminated off the cusp; amalgamated
one-by-one, into a heap of ash?

they were ego-busters citing their
curriculum of crimson-tinted value;
a syllabus of evil dust-cropping a crunch
of snide snickers as a people burned;
evildoers skimming the kingdom of inhumanity;

their state-of-the-art solution, final in its
scope, a tapestry of hate becoming a
fire-showering volcano; ruthless man-eating sharks
appraising their prey owl-eyed, voice shouting, booming:
who? who? who is next?

and now

the clapboard barracks stand,
receiving, grieving, in rows of silent chaperones,
stark naked and time-stained like so many reminders;

torture houses gone from pain to rot;
plagued as if by guilt, for standing idly by
as souls were trashed and thrashed and crashed
against the anguish of that stormy petrel,

and laughter stifled to a moan, pulsing
lifelessly through its own rubble; surviving
through filth and need and horror as some
undivided chill, that seems to spill and spilled into
the coming generation; stilled sparks of life, and
bodies intending to live still—but cannot... cannot...

time has made way for decay here, speared
into these lean-to consummated wooden carcasses
that bear witness for another reason...

gravel crunches underneath. dust rushes, settles
into something akin to a fissure—a cramped space that
only I can understand: as no place else to go.

it doesn't see me here at all...

easterly

the sun still rising reluctantly
above the bleak exposure,
seems to mourn the long-lost losses,
as it endeavors to devour the entire scene,
blinding me into thinking its fiery flicker
can ever hope to cleanse the blood
and tears and sweat and vomit
steeped deeply into this accursed ground,
by diabolical predators groomed to kill the
dreams that once-free men created;
by group-madness building monuments
to death and pyramids of mangled humans
sacrificed on the alter of foul ideals,
that still defend the ashes fashioned
by a contorted nation's blunder.

but amnesty is not forthcoming... nor answers...

the children of the Book died

not a whimper or a sigh left.
everything has happened; the people crowded
in the earth, not fitting squarely in their plots.
dead from fire and shots; their bones so weighty
and vast, there might not remain any more space here.

those who thought they will survive believed nothing
bad can happen anymore—or else couldn't see it:
the hungry earth, the endless dark, the long night
of another, deeper place. they come and come now,
and the children of the children, and still they die inside; the
past with its greedy eyes and grasping fingers seeking resolution
to the lusterless encountered.

watch, O greedy earth, the flesh gives in
to your nothingness, your zero, your negation.
they surrender, helpless, open to your grasp.
and the multitude of offspring give praises to
the dead, who are thought to sleep in peace when
the lights go out, thinking nothing bad can
happen anymore… but what s that ghastly
moaning wafting through
this meta-graveyard's umbrage?

burned:

burned by the Gestapo

burned by soldiers wearing
      crooked crosses

burned by willing volunteers

burned by hate

burned for keeping quiet

burned for speaking out

burned for being Jews

burned alive

burned dead

burned living/dead

burned for the sake of finding a "solution"

burned for the sake of Jew-purging

burned for the sake of genocide

burned for the sake of nothing

burned as if a generation was dispensable

cinders: skyward

burned into the hearts that conquered

ashes: scattered

burned bygone phantoms left to linger
      in the bloodstained ground
      on the smoke-stained sky
      haunting the murky pages of history

with the whole of me

I trek across the field of vanished flesh and
bone—the bones and teeth and hair of my people—
where death gloats over the ghosts circling
the semi-crimson terrain which witnessed slaughtered
dreams and humans, by glowering beasts tearing souls
from quivering flesh and canceled minds;

where the army of death tattooed numbers on
unwilling arms to snuff out any shred of dignity from
bleeding hearts; staunch intruders interrupting our journey
into fate, dishing out the worst that man can do to man:
doctors taking liberties of using living hearts,
subjecting them to vile experiments;
men, women, children scared of their own shadows,
shot and burned, beaten and ripped apart,
tortured into admitting they deserve it;
the smallest glimmer of light blocked out by fatal
strategies that dared declare wrong as right...

everywhere around

the ghosts of then
are seen with hands fused to foregone
faces with eyes that see no hopeful view;
souls who forgot their purpose
of embracing life without reserve;
aspirations chained to heavy boulders;blood and marrow forged
to bone,
refusing to agree
to living in despair;
to lost prospects;
to missing choices;

to tears frozen in their track
for fear of proving, back-to-back,
there's still a life to live
despite the paling faces in the absent mirror,
and the scorn that cuts into their being
like a Black and Decker
into living flesh...

many tried to hide

escape the groping
clutches of a nation-gone-mad;
hide from marching boots
and barking dogs;

"run…run…they're almost at my side…"

some persisted to survive awhile, interned
beneath some heaps of leaves for days;
afraid to move, even to breathe;
quit their breath to impossible proportions,
terrified they'd stir a leaf
into betraying their location;
scared that they'd return to run a bayonet
through their already lanced hearts;

but they were condemned
to take it from there without success—the
dogs found them and exposed their souls to
a slew of callous atrocities that washed away
all human dignity and worth… and life…

someone projects a wail

across the virgin of the silence, and the
unforgiving efface structures out a dread, and a
reverberation as an arsenal of empathy like a thunder poised
to pierce that unknown stranger; and the exhaled bolt
begins to rumble, pressing against the commonality
I call myself, slowly opening a stormy petrel of transference...

there is always a blast of ruckus from a sorrowed
visitor, an objurgated lexicon of hissed-out pain strewn all
around like some open wound attaching itself to anyone
in sight... but what about the buried souls?

I continue on my search

and feel the silhouette of death still overtly
lingering in the muted silence.
I look for footprints long ago receded,
and all I see is rusting barbwire fences
that were made to swallow fading egos,
ominously snaking train tracks breaking the monotony
of weeds, and hushed fields rampant with silent
memories clamoring for recognition;

under a generation of rot and dust and grime
I take note of the splintered barracks,
now blatantly sporting bare forsaken bunks
that cradled once laugh-prone finalists in
a game they had not agreed to play;
millions of doomed souls trapped
in a final contest of endurance;

under certain degrees of must and rust, I see
ruins of gas chambers, crematoria
that once gorged on living beings,
now shuddering at the memories they harbor,
of humiliated bare-limbed women,
vulnerable children and frail elders
wallowing in their own dregs and vomit, with
abandon plastered on their emptied faces,
later painted with the mask of death...

history declares them dead... but
not my conscience...

strange

that here, where human
cargo was replete,
that they could feel so all alone,
so world-delete—though
piles and piles of carcasses abounded,
and shouting SS cries, or sighing, pining
voices everywhere were founded;

but they were all imprisoned
in their blasted lot,
to live in a deadly snake-pit that the
world and fate forgot;
left balancing on destiny's barbed fence
with only fading, failing shadows as their friends;

forced to groveling for anything
that could be eaten, used;
their sanity compromised, reduced
into defending its existence,
and clinging at the death-throes
of a horrible subsistence
offering nothing but brain-drain
and soul-drain…

in those days

flesh was cheap;
the stench of death
filled the nostrils of quasi-life
with a pungent smoke that lingered
and festered in their marrow,
like a poisoned arrow
aiming to extinguish
all that they remembered
of bygone days,
and hopes meant to fly
instead of lying still and dead,
and weren't made to tread
on broken hearts
by love not fed…

what you saw

if you looked deep
into the clouded eyes
of those doomed souls,
was bleakness at its worst
and false bravado lost to dust;
but there was always
still a piece of the eye
watching out for number one.

they say that good intentions
last forever... theirs didn't;
they started out
as human beings seeking mercy,
and ended up as groping corpses
doing what was needed to survive—
some things questionable, to say the least—

and if one could hear the missing voices
of their once abiding souls,
one could faintly catch:
what about ME?...
what have you made of ME?... WHY?...

to some

it was a place that offered welcomed
numbness; a way to forget their unbearable losses.
to the rest it was Dante's Inferno;
a hell reduced to nothing less than hell's own
fiery graveyard, hot and smoky, full of rising ashes,
the hiss of evil tormenting the innocent with
inhumanities beyond comprise, and memories
of vanished pleasures lost in the corridors
of time—panic at its worst; robbed of pride,
trapped and raped and plundered,
forced to work long years (some too short);
to find a way to grieve children, spouses, kin,
without the benefit of tears—they couldn't
bear the thought of one without the other;

and if anyone should even dare to ask the
reason for their bitter slice, the penalty was
death by early incineration, or bullets
casting gaping holes through phantom
bodies holding nonexistent prides;

and so, on they trudged, numb and frozen to
their cursed present, left to apologize for still
surviving... until they surrendered to their fate...

in the loneliness of night

weeping souls reduced to heaps of
ashes could be heard regretting
their attempt at life;
during smoke-stained days demanding
nothing but despair,
the living dead remained silent—
yet anger still prevailed in some;

they longed to strike; to protest
against their fiendish captors,
bit-by-bit, to recall the ancient
right to be...
but fate destroyed their courage;
adversity, their inborn confidence;
heinous atrocities and famine, their strength;
the loss of loved ones, their living will
to try at surviving the living Hell
their world became: an all-or-nothing
living death that speaks only of itself...

in the dead of winter

the numbed toes and fingers
mirrored deadened hearts and souls
who forgot the art of crying.
crying was a luxury they couldn't keep,
and spare time an obvious deception;
so was familiarity or begging for help;

no one knew you there anyhow,
to hear your pleas
or help pass more favorably the time.
you walked an invisible line
between being and non-being,
without any delusions about
defining your lost identity;

sacrificed to the ruthless mauls
invented by a previously unknown enemy
who shattered glass windows,
burned sacred books and scrolls
and grabbed away the last tiny ridge
of sky left for sunshine to come through;
the smoke they furthered
smeared only darkness in its wake,
the heat melting away dwindling reserves,
which left ashes festering
in survivors' hearts and souls and minds
forever and thereafter...

they wouldn't close their eyes

for a minute, for fear their dream of flying
back to yesteryear would disappear;
they were afraid of everything;
afraid of shadows hiding between
the straw mattress and the splintered wall,
hoping they won't be seen, even in the dark;
going on like reoccurring nightmares.

everything is scary without hope;
they were even afraid to think, for fear
of being heard by their own
convictions to remain alive—
despite the whispers from their hearts;

later, all that was left was
wishing their hearts would go easy
on the hate boiling in their bowels:
their greatest fear-come-true was hate;

but hate sanctified their fear
and made it seem like
it was exactly what was needed to survive...

how they thirsted for happiness!

happiness???
they couldn't even remember what that was...
they had lost it so long ago.

it must have gone away to other places...
certainly not there!
not where hearts were blue, feelings
red and courage yellow!

not where the future was so bleak,
it was lost in the color of oblivion;
where hope was gray and outcomes hazy:
black as death can be
among the ashes scattered all around
on hopeless faces
and dying souls...

they begrudged the stance

those monsters took by force;
those devil's advocates
with self-made suppositions
to be far superior than they
who lived and died in silence,
bearing stoically their heritage
as if it spoke like quiet resignation
in the face of utter chaos, with hope
painted on stripe-pajamaed chests
crushed by man's inhumanity to man,
of ravishing the weak and strong alike
by bestial brutality and deprivation...

I guess it was in that hellhole snake-pit,
where hope became more dangerous than guns,
that they must have learned to hate,
and forgot how to love...

my father forgot only how to smile...

nothing in life seems free

to those enduring such a fate;
except bad times missing rays of promise;
except worries, once posing as abandon,
now turning yesterday's smiles
into today's uncanny whims prone to sadness;
except life sucked right out of living eyes
by flames turning brethren into ashes;
except heartaches hurting for a family
that burned, which happened to be yours;

except for welling tears
you try to shed for consolation,
but seem to dry before
you even try to give them leeway;
except strength and hopes and wishes
drained from your will to live;
except stumbling across stones
blocking thorny pathways, and years
that cannot suffer the right to be
when others were not granted such decree;
except lost loves, lost dreams lost beauty
that will never dare to see
the world again as it used to be...

I look and look

for some fitting explanations
to define the barefaced dehumanization
that once smeared this caustic place,
which suffered passions drained
by awesome ash and flames,
and chills impossible to savor;
I search for the holy key that will dismiss
this baneful emptiness I feel
in the hollow grotto of myself;

I strain and strain, but all I hear is the howls of
mad dogs hungry for disappearing shadows:
the living dead, or dead; stacks
of *figuren* piled and burned
on living pyres, next to mounds of gold
teeth pried out of dead Jewish mouths
and wedding bands from hands hardened
by death's grip; I try to peak my ears
for some sign that destiny regrets...

but all I hear is the deafening silence
sweeping through my soul;
millions of interrupted love songs
and stifled lullabies;
the wailing echoes tripped off
by a hundred types of horrors—
cruelties not of God's making—
the cries of wasted humans
sacrificed on a burning alter
that only boundless hate can fashion;
their blood staining this accursed ground
for a thousand years to come... and more...

how can you learn to want something

or take it for yourself,
if you re not allowed to feel
the deepest aspect of being;
stolen when you weren't looking
by some beastly hands
bent on erasing all that's left
of an already terminal condition?

yet, they did what destiny demanded
to survive the wreaking hazards...
except remember what they were once;

they were afraid to yearn for
the forgotten sill-life portrait
of their past, so their dream
would not be stolen from their hearts—like
all the rest; scattered in the wind,
along with the ashes left to linger
for eternity in souls
attempting to continue on...

as if their plight was not enough

they were plagued by lagging memories
of golden silky sands
with mist-kissed pebbles;
bronze horizons catching sunny rays;
salty seafoam spraying at their hungry eyes;
lapping waves that carry lacy seaweed
as a gift to sun-kissed beaches;
drifting clouds unmarred by smoke or ashes;

just shards of memories presented
to their weeping souls,
who begged for joys as they once happened;
these memories persisting as if
they meant to soothe their losses;

instead, they only speared bloody jabs
into their hazy, black-stained present,
becoming unseen arrows
wounding crusted hearts
that seemed to bleed with tears
not yet dried up by buried wishes...

they told themselves

that miracles still happen;
that prayers are still answered;
that pain may disappear in time,
replaced by quaint mirages
pretending to be lights of freedom;

but it never happened. even
God forgot to free His children
from the monstrous claws that captivated
living phantoms with minds and souls and
bodies right out of their existence,
and declared them perishable cargo;

muted hearts heaving beneath a brave facade,
their hollow cheeks were often tearstained;
the tears trailing deep fissures
that became, not so much the face of choice,
but the precondition to mortification
to a down-and-out scenario
that only death can verify...

although that furtive twist of fate

they did not plan or even fathom, each
of them was drawn to the darkness
of others, like a magnet
pulling at a chunk of steel,
hoping to merge their own
somewhere in theirs, so it can stain and
sting their hearts a little less;

the camp was packed full with
men, women, children, trying to endure,
but after a while, they buried
their dreams deep into
the ashes they discovered,
and concentrated on avoiding stains
that tend to last forever,
by pretending to be no one... yet
still surviving, striving, on and on;

until the century was made good—not
that the twentieth century was innocent
of marking numbers on people's arms
and sewing yellow stars on coat lapels,
but at least it gave them something to
remember, or forgive if they so inclined.

I guess no one ever could...

they prayed

oh how they prayed each day:
please dear God, lead me away from
this misery; let me no longer be enchained
by these mocking beasts; these evildoers who
wiped away all the smiles off my now faux face;
all the beautiful words, once loud and clear,
now silenced from my muted tongue ;

but reality set quickly in, sporting traces
of yesterdays that couldn't remain for long,
as long as happiness forgot its name
and scurried from despondent frowns
displayed upon a gruesome mask...
and a masquerade of souls paraded
behind obscure facades of papier mache
veneer that cast its hungry force upon their
ashen downcast faces...and their children's after...

hands white-knuckled and bone-withered

wringing out their ten degrees of grief;
their eyes a tapestry of pain, hearts erased,
they were mascots of the harbored hate

turning black and ash from the cremation;
eyes and teeth and souls extracted, pulsing
bits and pieces of themselves emptied
inside the hospice of the lathe;

sons of Cleaves dispatched by evil wattage:
gassed, harassed, burned, spurned
by a glacial-hearted monster:
talisman of the myth of demons;

fractured victims, ego-suctioned,
shuddering inside a live barb wire fence;
a final solution ruling the kingdom of hell,
emerging as survivors of the epic evil sweep...

as I proceed on

the mounting silence gave way to
shouts rising from the ashes left
behind from ghosts who linger still;
voices piercing through my soul,
so loudly, they threaten
to engulf it; this tortured soul
plagued by accumulated years of silence
from a father-heart that turned to stone

by a bitterness that sought and sought to fester,
seeking fitting reasons that the wrongs my kin
endured weren't sacrifices placed in vain
upon the alter of existence;

that forgiveness gleaned out of
the unmarked graves of millions,
may lend a helping hand to mend my soul
and stop this heavy mass
from turning to revenge… or worse;
from turning such a catastrophic tragedy
into a world-posted myth
that future children won't believe…

there's always one moment

even in the darkest hour,
when a door opens to let the sunshine in;
but theirs was bolted shut
by heinous men who threw away the key,
caught by a sunless world
that clutched it in its empty heart,
choosing not to use it...

left them to their sordid fate,
the good and the bad and ugly
living side-by-side;
the good beneath the crushing boots
of the bad and ugly...

the sun could never pierce through
the blackened smoke billowing upwards,
the clouds of ashes blowing in the wind
like a shroud covering a startled sky
coating their shrinking bones
and skin and jail-striped clothes;
staining their souls forever
and blurring their vision, which forgot
what pale-blue skies could look like;

while the other world around them
rolled on by as if it didn't owe that doomed
humanity a thing, except to stand and stare
and gloat and glare at what becomes a living
hell when men renounce to spread their
love on one another's fate...

but they lived to tell about it anyways...

each night

they d lay out their will to
live, to see if it was still there in
the morning;

sometimes it was not,
but their emaciated limbs
kept on walking to the beat of
mach shnell!!! ...
until one day the shouting stopped
and they remembered where
they left it hanging to be rescued;

but they were too weak to carry
it any further, so they hid it
back where it belonged: resigned
to merely seeking
reasons to survive a different kind
of hell...: the hell of living with
the recollections...

I try and try

to find the missing link that had chained them
to their dire destiny of being drained of their humanity,
blow-by-blow, as cruel fate and evil men would have it;
why hate stretches itself to unsavory limits when driven
by the lashing inhumanities that men contrive on the way
to meet themselves as they really are when stripped
of their integrity and good intentions;

brutal beasts that did not bear the burden of conscience
to lead them away from innate animal-like convictions. *but
even animals don't carry such vile attempts to their extreme,*
like those satanic demons wearing distorted crosses on
their armbands as if it were a banner of grand valor,
led by a madman screaming prejudice so loud, it hypnotized
a nation into committing unimaginably contorted crimes,
by sporting grandiose pretensions of being a *super race*
seeking *real solutions* in the winds of self-deception,
which fueled unforgivable flames of almost total genocide!!!!

by rights, it should be they, who bear such horrid losses!
they, who gained a life of ashes! they, who wear
their pains and guilt and stains of burned-in memories that
seek to snuff their bearers right out of being! they,
dispersed to a hundred empty places, missing roots and
nursing cinders of despair...

instead, it was their guiltless victims who suffered a major
detour from their intended fate, while their tormentors still
uphold within their lot the spewing tongues of unrelenting
hate that seeks to swallow the flailing remnants of their
blunder...

those mordant monsters

pretending to be men
defiled our scrolls, which history endorsed,
and our souls, that forever remorsed;
sucked the vitality from already phantom shadows;
corpses that once lived in their own shining truth,
condemned to moaning, groaning,
in barracks full of thirsting throats and hearts;
crammed in rows and rows of bunks, and led
like cattle to the slaughter; forced to bear the
choice of either dying a living death
or living a dying life...

they took away more than a body valued;
they robbed a being of the will to live!;
surviving barely, only because it saw no way out,
except continuing to uphold the Law of Life;
to live and let memories lead it to redemption,
by the decree of its people's prized commandments;
to live, and allow the only faux life possible after
such sordid harshness, to redeem the chronic loss...

what right did they have

those gruff magistrates
of death fascinated by all the ways people can die,
to deliberate their final solution and
fuel a holocaust of such inconceivable brutalities,
they wrote a story straight from Hades?
igniting flesh on fire, spewing souls
by the millions through gorging smokestacks
into darkened, stinking skies
towards the sunless horizon of oblivion,
while they laughed and jested
as the dying writhed and burned;
their haunting wails forever
banishing our peoples' true expanse;
to after dance the sordid dance of
the ill-conceived fate that they'd conceived…

they were the ones

who would not use their senses;
would keep them in reverse; would use their fists, their guns,
their smokestacks, all at the same time, to blacken any face
or race suggestive of salvation;

would be ill-advised to mourn their misconceptions, or
do anything needed to be changed; would collect rust and
dust and ashes upon their conscience, rarely shameful of their
deeds, and could seldom tell the difference between night and
dark, between right and wrong, between inhumane and human;

would appear on web-like patterns of their angst in the distance
of their hate, unaccountably unglorious and vain, showing
littleness of integrity, an about face nowhere to be seem.
all is diminished in this lacking world—though we love
it all, but hate each other; but what will the final hate
sound like when the last of love is buried, and the rest
cracked beyond redemption?

they handed an entire generation

(and countless generations after)
a fist of ashes to wear
on their lapels, like a yellow star,
as an unsuited attire of despair;
they sawed shrinking bones
and gnawed at disappearing flesh;
cut weeping hearts to shreds;
withered up a reluctant soul until it forgot
what it remembered of itself;

until it no longer hoped
to fathom life as it once
belonged to those who dared to dream,
and who no longer wished to see
tomorrow, if it be manned by hoary beasts
who can promote such spirit-breaking burdens
as if they speak of nothing...

they lived a dead life

when they returned to almost living;
they never figured out exactly why it happened;
only that they lost themselves along the way;

they lost their spark in those camps—but not
their souls—their souls wept on;
their tears to haunt the faultless minds of the
survivors, making their children the true victims;
casualties of a war they did not fashion or endorse;
children asking themselves... the world:

*how long before the fluid loss of phantom
voices stops haunting the days and nights and
dreams of generations yet to come?*

I wonder

did these crematoria chimney-stacks
spew smoke? fire? screams?

in which language did the screams rise
over tormented skylines?

on the skyline of this present dawn, which
tortured sighs does the wind repeat?

the tormented children's cries?
the men's? the women's sighs?

is there an ear more wide open to dismay
than the word genocide?
are there fangs more sharp
than the hatred of the beast?

tell those soulless bastards

who promoted their message of
hate, on their brutal quest of world-mastery, of those forgotten,
weeping children buried in the images of a dimly-lit past!

of evils too unthinkable for innocence and youth,
permanently staining their self-esteem, stifling screams
as they saw fathers snatched from their arms with empty
promises, turned them inside out, and released them to
the eternal silence of a total scream, as mere shadows
of the men they used to be;

fathers, whose voices were ripped from their throats, forever
stunted by the overlapping waves of inhumanity to man,
leaving them as hazy shadows moaning and shuddering
through
drenching nightmares; walking ghosts who forgot the art
of living, buried in the mire of despair and guilt;

tell the children they conceived why they were robbed of
their true legacy, left in the arid wilderness of deprivation,
lacking portrayal, and searching for unanswered questions;
walking alone as they seek a final closure through
the scorched land those evil mongrels left behind;

children weeping because none of it makes any sense; crying
because the world has already forgotten atrocities that washed
away all human dignity, all words from the faultless minds
and hearts and souls of a century of fathers...

I look around me

and all I see here is a godless place...
and think: so what if God still walks, after all—as
walk and walk He must, if He's to also find some
valid explanations—on this sorry piece of real estate,
cutting with his gaze into the cre(m)ated emptiness
from every angle, scanning for some light still clinging
in a careful manner to the grotesque transformation,
making every stab count in His direction,
until the eyes of man are fixed on the blue air
of His papery-thin suspension? so what?...in
that goddamned then, He made himself absent—even
from this; this cruelest of places;

maybe this God we so eagerly await, or look to,
makes Himself invisible, more transparent than wind,
to suffer the most daring life there is: anonymity
in magnetism and stillness, existing only in cathedrals
filled so intensely by pugnacious nonbelievers,
like an immense presence pressing into empty spaces...
and no sound or grace in the transparency at all;
feeling pity the moment we cry out in pain,
but still content to never make Himself discerned...

and the silence slips past us,
and all we hear is a harsh hush, and all we see
is a blind eye fixed on the ceiling of the endless sky,
and a vow to remain anonymous...

we've won! !! we're free!!!

they cried,
we survived the least of it...
the smallest of our plight;
the worst is yet to come:
living with our survival;
the guilt that we persisted
when others didn't;

and seeding a generation of children
paying for their fathers' sin
of living on; for forwarding the memories that
taunt our nights and make our days
a living nightmare—that part is harder
than the blows a dying body takes ;

they were told to go home. **home???**
where was home? who was home?
just a people scattered
to the four corners of the world: North,
South, West and East, to that land
of milk and honey... **home!!!**
(where other beasts were waiting furtively
to snatch whatever wasn't snatched before...)

but home it was!!!
is this the justification?
or merely fate apologizing for its folly?

give us a chance

they pleaded from their vessels of despair,
with nowhere else to turn but back to nowhere; *a chance to*
prove that we deserve acceptance; deserve to live; a chance to
resume our ancient journey from the land of no return;
show us that some caring still exists in other men's intentions;
that nations still own hearts willing to rescue a people
from their darkest hour; to restore them to the dignity
their honorable heritage demands;

that the world has not forgotten the forgotten; that
humanity will remember the unremembered; will repay the
valuable gift of conscience freely given by their LAW, which
graces worthy constitutions everywhere that freedom lives;

take us in! redeem yourselves from staying silent
while we screamed for help and reeked of burning flesh!!!

alas, so few donated their consent to embrace a homeless
cargo seeking mercy of their fellows… the many
failed miserably again, again, their timely test….

looking for a speck of logic—

surrogate at least—lingering among
the ashes left behind, I hurl a sudden-impact-sort-of-question
towards selected segments of the phantom-windreach of the
absent sky: why does the earth gulp globs of flesh, making men' s
pure souls rot in her mud, leaving only a Morse-code bitterness
residing in the rootless acetate of later; a few dead dreams, and a
layer of mordant frowns (inconsequential, according to the masses)?

surely, the earth, nor its sky, can't want bones, marrow, hair,
eyes, stretches of charred skin, the breathtaking scope of smiles?
and yet it chews up and swallows heart-songs; and a
myriad of faces stripped of life bear it to the point of chasing
rainbows that aren't even there anymore— molten flames ranged
in a range of stippled combinations manifested out of hate.

we stumble into musty graves—not even of our making— and
the earth
reaches for the heart no longer fibrillating life... and she is
satisfied?
though she rewards us with a satire of flowers sometimes, this
is the misshapen in her: the monstrous creatures she devised.
we can swagger on a comet's tail all we want, before she turns
us into rot; yet resident upon the ground, in sea or sky, for us, the
final frontier is the hollowed earth... and there are those who
further
her intent: the beastly jackals who have built this abomination.

how many dynamic shocks can a people pretend to bear and
be still certain they exist?; span a litany of atrocities plucking
at the strings of silenced voices, and still pretend they matter?
I guess this is the cruel, the harsh in her, this earth: that under an
eiderdown of annihilation, there still are those who feign
survival...

explain to me

how a world could continue on its course;
could carry no remorse
for dissipated dreamers,
and find still-vivid souls expendable?
how it can turn a frigid shoulder
to grief-stricken almost dying faces;
snuff already waning candles while the sun's
still shining, though their light is disappearing fast?
build strangling fences out of barbed wire,
when all they do is swallow broken hearts?

how they can split open ancient hearts
and suck out every drop of life left,
causing death-by-life and life-by-death?
and then, how the others, closing their hearts to the
survivors of such unimaginable cruelties,
can still refuse to let them in when there is
nowhere else for them to go?

how ordinary people marching onward
to their own impending graves,
can endorse the tragedy of endings
as if they had nothing to do with it?

explain this thing called apathy...

interesting

how some people stumble into something like a
horrible malaise, following… what order? what war?
walking into blindness with a deep-rooted seat of hate in their
ego-laden chest; or go on with a shrug, when others are being
burned to cinders. they try—or not—to quash the flames, but
cannot move their limbs in time. so they begin to look for a cure.
they find it in a scapegoat they envision as an enemy, cup it in
a box of ash; a bleeding error carrying a flag.
then, there are those who avoid the harrowing events by hiding in
a shallow shell—something like a holy sepulcher of coveting the
land—even if it isn't theirs; an accident of birth, all clash and dash.

interesting how they hunger for a veil to bury under, waiting
for the madness to dismantle of its own accord, turning their
heads so cocksure, the way a head is buried in the sand, playing
chicken little to the sounds of wailing children trying to
wade into a sea of calm— even as the world burns, again
and again and again to the thunderclap of Taps—tired and

down-smitten, rising out of the ashes like a defeated phoenix…

they emerged as fallen heroes

to be overshadowed by the bailed-out
semi-victors, who apologized by certain sums,
trying to redeem the world they created
and attain a measure of forgiveness.
I wonder if such a meager token can
cancel out the criminality that rendered
human beings into ashes?

**goddamn it, you cannot buy forgiveness
with a monthly check!!!**

it cannot wipe away the lingered ashes
from the living dead, or off
that bloodstained ground of their demise, to
spring a river of content; can't erase the
rancid taste of anger left on severed tongues!
can't awaken dormant nostrils that forsook
a rose's fragrance, and dried-up lips
that had forgotten how to smile!
the ciders are too deeply furrowed
in survivors' flesh and blood and souls...

all they could muster up, was a false
bravado pretending to be a faint *thank you* ...
their grim reality strains to whisper in their
ears, that embers made from smokestack pyres
can never be extinguished by merely
throwing restitution vouchers at those who
no longer exist in their own selves, but
in a past that vanished with their youth,
reduced to living a life resembling death...

or their torpid children...

I'm sure

their mothers taught them many
useful things:

how to deal with pain and strife;
with hard times birthed by life; with making
do with less than nothing— they proved that—
but what they forgot to teach them,
was how to deal with this inner sorrow;
this wasting emptiness formed by ashes
remaining still, staining injured hearts
once treated as nonexistent specks
of dirt beneath the boots of SS guards,
forced to listen to their insults as their
spirits were broken up into knifelike shards;

didn't teach them how to journey through Hell
whistling down the wind of fear, or how
to avoid sowing lasting tutelary seeds of hurt
into their children's hearts and souls and dreams;
nor how, as living phantoms, they can erase
the lie: it never happened —or bear it...

but to the ones who feel the soot
smeared heavily upon their doleful souls,
the reality of being here
after surviving hell on earth,
bears the mark that only truth can carry...

and the lesson has been fully learned...

a generation

versatile and ancient
had their dream cremated
in those death-camps,
by beasts who hated
people into ash.
and now their children
are numbed, mummed,
hung up and strummed;
causing them to feel
with skull and spine
and not with heart and soul.
did either the hater
or the hated feel
the scalding breath of death
plotting interjection?
or did they each straddle
the black perimeter ignoring
the surreal tide of ingrained fury?

and I, a survivor too, somehow,
stand back and watch
how the amalgamation
flares out from the center
of the ashes as a
genetically engineered facade;
the remnants with a harsh patina
remembering in their genes the
multitudes who perished...

they say the dead don't talk

but as I stand here in this god-folorn
place, in the still-echo-land that suffered cries
of dying men and crying souls,
impotent and deaf towards their plight,
I think I hear them sighing in the wind
of their wish to be remembered,
and not be stashed away
into the frozen ground of the forgotten—
that land of no return—as a compendium
of lingered ghosts whose bodies were
scattered all around the blackened
ground, with unseen scabs that welcome
only time to cry against the sky, to sigh into the
wind, until the day we all will die with
no one left to speak of their existence;

but their silenced voices
won't be heard at all;
death, with its deleting kiss,
made sure that they
will never be missed;
for it took away the very ones
who would remember...
but not me... not me... I remember... remember...

too many of our children

were rendered into soap;

too much of our women's hair
filled their mattresses;

too many of our corpses
smeared their bloodstained soil,

their darkened sky,
too many tons of our ashes;

their smoke-stained clouds
that will remain that way
as long as hearts remember...

and I aim do it
by shooting tearstained words
towards some paper stars...

dear God:

how many died?
how many murdered?
how many cremated?
those shot at? knifed or strangled?
those enslaved and vanquished?
the brave who were shot in rows of thousands?
how many children who dreamt of being born
murdered in the womb?
ten? a thousand? a million? more?

how about the babies experiencing that
constant war? the uncaring flames?
how many hurled their last cry
as they lay dying? only one? or a thousand?
lying in the reddish-purple like a flowing river?
how many Abrahams and Iacovs and Rebeccas
must have perished,
dissected of their blood-rich dreams?
how many made their way to you?

oh yes, the bombed-on civilians?
the slain masses going about their tasks?
the innocents? the wronged persons?
did you see any of those?
how many Jews, clueless of their fate,
shot in pogroms? starved in ghettos?

or perhaps the martyrs, the Warsaw ghetto
uprisers, the rabbis, the women? the teens?
and can you tell us: if you can be in two

places at the same time, were you there
when they were gassed?
and did you see them laugh as
they turned the children into ashes?

really, six million is a lot... you must have
met some of them up there, dear God...

with daylight dimmed to a faulty blush

I peer into the fading yonder, the dark archaic body
of light-turned-dim so I cannot see them there;
the former life-forms floating in that silent frond.

all I can see, is that the day failed into a twilight that will not
be calm or cool or lit; just a loosening of shriek-spanned dark;
millions of dead souls, still alive and wise and vibrant,
drifting in a macroscopic sea of dust-spores, scattered with their
past fanned around them, like life-lenses pulled tight, sharpening
and blurring the focus over the shadowy pit of their restless shades,
fire and ashes radiating, the curdling screams impossible to quash.

and suddenly I know: souls appreciate the fine edges of a delicate
existence, not being trapped in the breast of a survivor's child
straining in vain to sleep, to disengage from the paining multitudes,
looking back over their idle shoulders to see if someone can remember;
waiting, bearing the burden of their blunt demise. all they want
is a heritage of children to approach the proximity of this graveyard
with an ancient prayer of condolence... not a legacy of endless tears
poured out in their name... there is never anyone there...

as the sun glowed somewhat golden off the far horizon, I
continued to the gate, and dusk began to blur the line between
what whips past and what remains to haunt us, to engulf the
mind
and settle on a total shout that lasts forever. yes!!!
I know now: this can only come to some good;

I will no longer feed the monster...

I look back:

the barracks are empty
the neat rows of cots reeking must
shy away from the barbed coils
rusted into static silence,
the muted watchtowers
penetrating the sky
like a fist against the killing;
every cry from
flesh and blood and bone
now silent;
cells and tissues and hearts
cremated mute
rise as an immensity
against the arsenal of shame;
the survivors scattered
across the globe;

a generation trying to revive
a more favorable past from dust;
trying to survive
the sash of ash
clinging like a hardened crust;
striving to build castles on
the cusp of trust;

but what's left of a dream
after the flame? after the scream?
can it ever be the same?...
yet look, there; out of the dust
the heritage endures,

as hope, as life, as multitudes
revived from dying cinders.

and the child whispers anew;
committed to shops and stocks, to
bricks and stones and mortar. but
alas, again the flames arise, fanned
back to life by the cunning beast...

with dusk anemic substitute for daylight

bobbing on the river time, I fade into its haze,
and I become a stranger to the new parameter; a
prodigal daughter, even a pariah for having come in the first
place, becoming one with coming night, to suffer the most
daring death there is, the most viral; a death that makes of the living
a prey that only it can bear—not them; inept sieves trying to filter out
the relevance of the past, the limn of alpenglow threatening to sink
evenly into the gossamer of the now, wishing only to be swallowed
up as is, taken in slowly, with careful thought; as stretched
across the
dark as a factor ambling through the fuzzy augmentation,
resilient to
the vermilion transformation needed to continue; ever wishing
to be threaded through the new next day, born again at sprouting
intervals as a simplistic definition, intricate, complex, not mucid,
undefined.
tomorrow is another day;
a gust of sudden wind stirred the dust;
to me it sounded like a rushing whisper: *come back… come back…*

I've come here to grieve

the necessity of mourning, rethink the loss-tide,
its nightly waning, ebbing; respite then reprise, giving in,
protesting, the moon pulling the strings like a giant puppeteer;
to stop pretending I don't have a choice in withstanding the past
storm spiraling inward until every second will condense into
itself and burst into a red flame saying *no* to going on.
this is a long-awaited day, open
to the blue of itself, the Olympic mission, the wet that tears make,
centered and spent as if in a lassitude of solace; they are nothing but
seductions
on the pathway of delusion; a layaway plan that keeps on weeping
for a soft and tender release, never satisfied till all of me is
spent dry, made intangible by a harsh consolidation.

I tell myself repeatedly to treat the world as a thing to still forgive,
to smooth it into place and think it as a matter that recedes into
its own logistic when ignored into inconsequence, into the hard
copy of
another time, a series of slots and aphorisms on either side of midnight.

so as I stand here with my feet at the edge of this blood/ash-
stained terrain,
plugged
into its dimming horizon, watching the sky wing its way
towards extinction, I want to shout: *hate and hate…and so little
love!!!… go home!! don't linger here. don't continue, or
you will dissipate before
this place of shame apologizes! write your thing before you disappear
in the vernacular…
there are empty pages to be filled; and how empty they remain*

*when no one lays some secret at their feet, a surge and ebb
towards the celebration of today; the inextricability, the
sufficiency of living and living on despite the pain.*

*they killed them, and there is no other way to mourn that loss:
that splendid gift of you inside a meaning. this is not about the world
they left you in, the catastrophe it has become without you and your
wings and the right*

*to who you are, and the purpose of this treck—it
is about the current that tugs you, in spite of you, to the center of
yourself, the shadow calling you home to the absolution of total
forgivance; away from the milkweed of oblivion where you live now,
as if it were a death, calling…calling…*

*it is there, in that velvet of yourself, you must remain, tangled in your
own poem, deep in the flow of tides and lines and the ascot tie of
belief still in humanity; and as the thunder comes, like Satan's voice,
to make them
inane, these pulling tides; inconsequential. no more splintered
songs, and grief for you… just a sort of coming home.*

I see it: a curtain has opened, ever so see-through sheer; and it
gladdens me…
I will go on…

I feel the cold and windy desolation

creeping right into my marrow.
a shadow following me around tries
to break itself away from the rest in me... in
vain, for there it is, right in my heart,
seeing me for who I really am:

a vagabond traveler seeking to dispel
ashes left behind to linger in the souls
it covered up with soot, so dark,
they and she, forgot life is meant to further
its own purpose, and not to languish
in the dark corridors of the past;

and that tomorrow is a better day,
and earth consumes whatever man
tries to bury in its welcome caverns,
if only we allow the ghosts to pass away
from ruminating consciences
into becoming the walking dead...

suddenly, this hellish sort of plot

becomes a place to leave;
the droplets forming on my brow
and tears that stain my resurrected face
are dripping like a gushing spring
splashing their gold and russet spray
over my entire being, cleansing me,
begging me to dive and bathe into its flow,
so the past won't turn it into crystal puddles
that threaten to drown the rest of what is left
of my attempt at moving on;
where ashes left to linger in my heart
to sear it black as long as it continues
beating to the time of wasted life, are washed
right clean by the drip-drip of these tears—at
least into pretending it forgot; remembering
only that what is not, is; and what is, is not,
and cannot mar my conscience any more...

this is not a woman's duty…

but it doesn't mean
a thing when you've rammed inside yourself
incredible new rules.

who else? who else has earned that right?
who's been scattered to this mournful wind? who
has a piece of me left buried in this odious graveyard?

who else here to utter that solemn cry?
that prayer meant to lay at rest the souls of the departed,
and the souls who try survive?
who else is here? no one else but me yipping at the sky.

I open the Book. hear myself exhale the Kaddish:
Yit-gadal V yit-kadash Sh mey Raba…

they will hear… they will forgive…
they will release me…

the light begins to dim

the shadows of a
grisly past glide by as if unseen,
but deeply felt within still.
day has almost left the deathly quiet; only
the silent skyline with all its constant dread
remains, as night struggles to conceal the
object of its contempt;

only the dead remain to tell me
they will never really die, not as long as I will
live to give them life in my flight of fancy;
loved ones, who once were here, now spirits
dissipated to the wind, their souls striving
to resist my leaving them alone to whisper
into absent ears.

shivers run up and down my spine as I hear
them pleading softly to my heart, that more
of us should come to justify their being prone
to ashes left to linger here, alone.

I pass on by. I take a final sigh, and for the
last time I say good bye to the once-portent field
that nightmares furnished; while just a scant few
miles away, well within the range of hell's remains,
the music is horribly alive, and restaurant signs
boast their best attempt at an apology:
the best apple strudel.

I don t feel like hearing concerts or eating
anything right now...how can I? crammed
full with ghosts that will not leave me... until
I write the story of their plight?

a haze of rising souls,

and then again falling, and once more rising
to the sky, only again to fall; and fallen, wait and only wait
to be resurrected once again—but alas, they keep on
falling, falling, getting furrowed deeper, deeper in the ground;
trodden under beneath the trotting feet of hordes of mourners,
returning, coming here to pay respects, soon to be gone
for good; gone and never once to rise...

for now, they fall and fall again; rising—which they must,
if they're to fall once more—they linger in the air; that fatal air;
but only for a faint minutiae, a fleeting instance, and then
again, that falling... falling; that thunderbolt, that dark shiver
of a crash to earth... and gone away for good, and no more
rising... no more rising... no more falling, falling...

genocide

washing away
a whole generation
slaughtered
burned
mangled

slandered
scorned

secreted mute

patricide
matricide
infanticide

appalling
horrid

best remembered
not forgotten

back in the taxi

I wonder: oh, why is it, everywhere I look, that this hazy
evening in this liable land, reminds me and reminds me
yet again of their ghosts, see-through like some elusive fog;
the way they are forbidding, unforgiving for the casual response
the world offered to the outright cruelty they bore... the way
the
Aryan beasts stole their sun and they were lost among the
cinders, or as have-beens in a pond of human ashes...?

once before, for just a passing moment in that place of guilt,
I also felt it; felt I could compose something like a shroud of
sadness as a testament to the paradox of that time: that
of being both full of promise to some, and empty of a life
at all, by those turned into ashes; to questions more harrowing
than vainglorious... and in the still of midnight, this poet
will somehow write their sorrow in some weeping poems...and
they will know the stolen moment of their stifled voices has
returned to me; is heartfelt against a full surrender of lasting
words; and after, when I'll come to wander on that desolated
ash-field once again—as come and come I must—I'll clasp
hands
once more with them for just a silent instant, and the poem will
vanish like a heart's hollow whisper, and the shade of me that
voices verses will became a modified caesura; immolated,

knowing exactly how bruised these ghosts must be, and why
their tender silence seemed an answer to my search for
closure...

in the dark silence of a dead synagogue

below the lacuna of an ancient ark,
I have brought my soul here to this house of
God in a guilty land,
to bear witness to a frenetic past

of bent old men of then wearing prayer shawls,
bearded patriarchs mouthing chanted prayers,
now just stained memories plastered on the
crumbling walls, forlorn by even time;

broken dusks of centuries of flapping twilights
reduced to wisps of ashen gray and sepia brown
by those god-loving shadows forced to flight,
now brought back in graphic detail

in the pale of amber light of coming night;
and I have brought a wailing poem
to recite among the ruins...

a jew's prayer

"you are my chosen"

**why would we want that??? gunshot and flames
and sharp tongues are biased!!!**
then the multitudes—tarnished, human, vulnerable,
assorted historic atrocities unfolded right before them,
dropped to their knees, each praying:

"may I never be born as a Jew next life, or after"

and in the distance, a rumbling could be heard... a peal
of thunder... a pulled rug... or was it laughter?...

in the aftermath:

we, the children of a lesser fate

seem to be invincible;
though tortured, burned and scorned,
we somehow still survive with dreams alive,
despite the daunting blows we suffer.

it boggles the mind how some tortured souls
can still find that sacred place within
that hosts the spark of hope, which should have
perished in the surreal experience endured,
grab control of life by its better side again,
and create a new one for themselves,
where none could ever be devised by others;

it blows me away how some injured hearts
can bring new children into a world
that traumatized their bygone families into oblivion,
subliminally teach them to embrace
the world, and somehow turn a legacy of
despair into a dedicated service that staunchly
seeks a way to mend that world...

I aim to be among the ones that do...

hate, I deny you, defy you;

you cannot taint my spotless
blood forever with your harsh
demands to wipe the solid peace
originally instated in my ancient genes;

to encourage me to ravage souls
with your belated poisoned spear,
until every drop of love is denied
and the last resolve is disempowered;

replaced by grief
attempting to haunt all my days,
and hope and life erased
from my concerns...

I used to be a ripe volcano

waiting to erupt;
anger spilling over the top
right into my altered cells,
to burn like ashes left to smolder
on a darkened soul,
who sought to see the day
but could not find the light;

the smoky film
emerging from the recess,
veiled my eyes and heart and dreams,
turning hope into a mound of wasting soot
and useless dust
reminiscent of the blackened sky
surrounding moonless nights
bemoaning fates of absent futures;

someday soon,
when my heart is full,
and love emerges from the dim horizon
in the guise of parity,
laughter will replace the genetic frowns
cursing through my veins,
bringing forth a happiness
that cancels out the sorrow...

ashes left to linger

the point is to roam into the concentric crux of it and
come out with something to share; a slew of resurrected
phrases, a nest of poems hummed like a redemption.

you listen to inner echoes rattle their list of protests,
but you choose instead to use them as an opening,
a start of something new, something vivid, not livid.

there are a thousand ways to describe it, but only one
conclusion to draw before the dark curtain falls
upon your eyes and earth embraces your facsimile.

some of the sharpnesses will dissolve, others will hold
on for dear life, then fall by the wayside in a future
epithet of ripe juxtaposition.

nonetheless, you'll know it, you'll feel it; that yarn, that
satellite of verses starting to spin their magic. you'll
fill the pages, color them, first gray,

then red, then pink, and feel that stir inside, that
hint of life still glimmering, along with the ashes
left behind to linger, flickering out a new momentum…

if just for an instant

could the wind of the past,
turned hard and harsh and dry, not engineer an
inward mutilation? there used to be nothing but
the howl of windshear, furtive as a glut of twitches
heading for my dark place—the place that has a bad
smell to it, and a worst feeling, also pointless...

oh, how our dreams surrender when surrounded by
that troubled air. phantoms still? yes. what does
it encode? that they have all become blood messages
in stone to leave far behind; changed into something
time has spent years concealing; forget-me-nots to
pluck later on and pile into some blooming phrases,
verses, poems... and continue on as someone healed;

a member of the present, able to conciliate on a
precision curved around the each of every day;
certainly not the product of memory it becomes,
too foreign for anyone to feel anything at all
but the bone-chill of their constant presence...

who hears the cry

when the poem arises on a field of blind paper?
its words and stanzas bled into a question-mark bouncing off
the pure-white vellum tundra? who blinks? who even weeps?
who bleeds at the vision that the poem already limns? scaly scabs
lining the pages, squeezing aside to make room for change. what are
these words in their chosen form? are they from a past that will not
fade; their sighing in the writing reminding us they still survive?

before I was born, the glow of fickle ease fell off and a grim sheath
settled on the century, the rush of hours bypassing this side of
laughter. I searched the vastness washed since clean by rain, fossils
in stone shriveled beyond recognition by the black hand of
time, but
all that could be seen is the dull ache of survivors, living a rusted
blue beginning encapsulated in solid rock. a full crock of sh.. hitting
the airwaves, burying the beholder and his offspring in its dregs.

now who writes the poem? is it just a tumbling tumbleweed
blowing in the arid desert; sharp and thirsty and brittle, rolling
for miles in the miracle of a dust-storm that will send it to a waiting
poet, to be found by her hungry fingers and mounted on a page, where
blood seeps out from behind thorns? no! it vanished a long time ago!

but still the solid pang remains. which words to use? heroic? or echoing
at the speed of pain, appearing now and then in a phrase designed

to keep the lethal chained, the silenced squawking, reverberating into
a need to paste the world together, meld it into decades of peace in the wake of a harsh and bloody past?

sometimes I think nobody but me can tell this story

the same old story, again and again; seems to drive people wild. these words are good for nothing but punching out pule. ten hours in front of Windows 2000, and I just want to puke; make some phrases do something beautiful for a change.

every day the same old crap; retold stories over and over again; the same fingers up and down and sideways on the keyboard, gesturing a lifeless mouse around with nothing to show for it except a story to be told at the end of the day to someone willing to listen; a friend, a mate, a paper tundra.

how much are we worth anyway? inside we all have a red light telling us to stop, move away from the lousy computer; from the narrow space we live in where, if you close your eyes, you can pretend it's not a sameness turned against you; pretend you're anywhere else but where you are.

I promised myself I'd quit focussing on the past, but yesterday keeps on calling my name… and whoever heard of walking away clean anyway? not after everything's already screwed; not after your world is tarnished by its own excreta, the droppings affixed to your footprints the way a dump of dung sticks to your shoes when you step into it; the way it keeps on piling higher, higher, closer, closer… suffocating everything trying to survive…
hey!!!! take a nice, deep breath; breathe though this paper bag… there is no bag, no breath… nothing survives.

(unrest)

early morning. lake calm. frogs announce it is time
to leap forward. to forget. but out of the envelope memory,
all I see is an incomprehensible past hovered in its own
white blood; the shape of what I'm not, against the
curve of world-madness and its regret.

are those ghosts of humans rising out of the lake?
pelagic, repine phantoms murmuring in sotto voce
of a void Elysium they have not gained?

I do not question what I see, but what I feel; what
needs to come to light, to probe, to be unmistaken for a
forfeit; to rehash what needs to rise out of the scarred
horizon of a bygone world gone mad (still mad);
to shout: rise from the moon's ashes, you, of the
petrel silence of a total scream; you, who rose out of
the cinders, resort not to merciful forgetting, but
merciful retelling and again retelling; not humming
apologies for the permanent stain of the sin of birthright!

I keep asking: was it madness to try circle the fire of stars again?
madness to try dance on the past's grave?
drag its remains off with monstrous human claws, flawed,
pithy claws, and let that monster rest? not replace it with a
terrible darkness; the darkness of living with the harsh

recollections, not even mine and mine alone to claim; the dark
of flesh against flesh being shaped as it goes as far as a
still-breach; a polarity of survival.

late last night, always secreting rivers of secrets, fingers
spindling out a shared regret, I gave in, writing fierce and
long of how my people lived so fine before the demons

spewed their fire into gassing ovens... we called it fate
when death-cries emitted from the dying went unheard, and
we succumbed to someone else's cruelty; yet we endured...

yes, we endure, we even feign a measure of ease, even
as we write of it, or not....and still we'll rest unrestful
beneath the sod...

after the life-modifying trek

a gathering of
old memories receded to the background,
somewhere deep inside where they can't be named,
an overwhelming lot now trying to rush to the background,
by the journey mellowed, by time yellowed,
by the falls it took and stumbles halted, tamed,
filed away in the place I've chosen to call home;

where recollections billow in the spangling past-dust
like gauzy bits of stored factoid
trying to avoid the cruelty of manifestation;
the penalty of living too long
in the all-prevailing dark of time's fantastic storage bin,

where harsh mementos sigh a long and wistful breath-hush;
where frequent expirations whisper in the moment's rush,
and old remnants lap oneiric at the edges of our space,
trying to imitate a favorable candle-flicker
dancing in tandem with the love-light in your life.

where a moonlit channel reflects its game-plan
to extend this present season; to dot the present warmth with
charmed delight; try to spark my inner embers into
resurrection,
turning them into a comforting poetical desire

to shape the details of the remainder of the day with the
red-ochre of October-breath, a glowing ray

pulsing with the unfamiliar passion that was once inbred;
in this place of me where elongated frowns turned into a lapse of
smiles; where lives a royal fest of outstretched life-play;
where love's glissando kaleidoscopes its pompatus
into the panorama I have personally arrayed, and my lover's
arms are blessed umbrage, umbrage, constant, warming, never-tiring;

there to fear nothing;
there to release myself with gentle fire;
for there I can fully be my lover's,
forever…

all is fuzzy and still-life now

and the past hardly exists; the heavyweight
of it, the full-blown aspect of its orientation,
the hiss and frown of it, the adaptation
unmeasured against the brilliance of the present
splayed on almost-better days;

the dual silk or rough boucle of it—even on the
frequent shadows with eyes poised
towards corruption; proxysms
stopped in their track by shouts and whispers
too loud to ignore.

I came to see, after that fateful trek,
that the past will invade any territory,
just to get its way,
fitting in quite well into the milieu,
all-prevailing and frequent in one's flight;

and that I need to go on, to survive—
and mostly I do—by following in the footsteps
fated ahead of me, one after another,
up/down an unlikely hill, a rock, a mountain-range
or under its shadow…

an echo

I offer a
disquieting echo
of myself
raised as a roar—my own—
against the absurdity of scorn's blurry
upside-down contortions;
my aging hand
trembling
out a pule in the darkness
of a dwindling day,
slamming out a quiver, a sorrow
disguised as verse;
black smudges competing with the
opaque tumult,
realized deep in the voice of me;

a thundering surrender
of unquenchable thirst
for waves of truth and love to manifest;
a soul-searching for magical solutions;
a sea of golden rhythm
dancing out a harmony of peace;
ticking out a song
that might call my name into
a reverberated hope of a more fit tomorrow,

connecting me to oceans of
trembling possibilities;
a floating silence
as fluid as time itself,
waiting... waiting... to materialize.

little time is left me

I have to leave to the next tyranny
my yammering poems,
like a proclamation—an antenna
appealing to all manner
of opinion; an abundance equally able
to feed both saint and sinner, to leave a lasting

mark against the wind and the void it forms;
voices of the fury, bellows of the screeching
roars from deep within the earth, the great
confusion, bits of me cut up and planted on
the ground, set loose into the sky to fly home;

how else can I rouse myself from the grave?

the old carry memories like stones;

call it heavy, shape it to an imperfect
fit on their shoulders. all recollections
that fill their brains, stop the living,
replacing it with gray hunger; turn to
pumice that rubs against the marrow.

hunger is a state of mind, they say;
a memory is just a memory, a part of you;
you cannot peel it off the bones
because you've gained the years, each
new one added to the pile swelling
in the gaping distance of a daily sky.

the farthest stone is just another rocky
layer on one's no-longer sturdy bones;
that stone is now glued with borrowed
time: that mocking nothingness
that only blank skies can understand;

every remembered boulder that offers to rob
me of another choice; every rock flaunted at
my waning flesh, makes only sense to death,
waiting eagerly to rewrite my story,
turn it into an unhappy ending;

every time another stone is added,
I meet with more of them; become
more powerless to reinvent my present;
becomes part of this pile of rocks,
growing… growing… into a mountain
of perpetual hunger…

(through with the past((?)):)

suddenly my attempt to spill myself into today seems to dig a
cruel grave for phrases, a crypt for everything that took me to this
moment, winding my way from a funked-up childhood, to this;
this harsh pretense at being a pardonable past.

I played a critical part in that journey. the agony and ecstasy of it,
too copiously elongated in my shadow to ignore, made me
wonder
if the sobering, less flippant agent moving between my fate and its
equivalent, time, was the potential trap handed by such newly
piebald bitter-sweetness. is it just an impediment to the life it bore,
that plagues this poet, or is it simply trickles of discontent?

in another time, I'd rant and rave and roar; I'd find a secret
slope among the golden words; that wisdom-bud that tends to bloom
whenever darkness will allow, those burning thistles jutting from
the deepest blueprint of my ID; bask in the glow they point to, and
howl, bellow, ululate, point their heroic vestments to an
alabaster
tundra, or paint them across a darkening horizon… but the
pule of
total silence has settled in and filled the colossal gap…. oh, give me
a taste of it now; that boiling blood that must be brewing there!
but no! silence is the miracle that shows up instead… and I'm
ever so grateful for the gained reprieve…

though I feel death nipping at my bones, the voices have stilled since, the poems have become more gentle. I guess I'm not too old to send some shining poem forward from the cave of me—one that will depict this dark garden as capable of giving birth to beauty... because it says
I am alive still... and I am... I am...

eventually

a frequency of nightmares
becomes a burden
we can bear,

releasing a deeplly-buried
cache
of dreams that now
survive them;

allowing briefly-glimpsed
reflections
of a past that yearns
to build and guild today
anew,
with an array of vindicated rhyme

as the sum of summons in our
heart pretends
to be an reference we endorse...

epilogue

recently, in that land of fault and blunder, a book,
then film, attempted to portray Hitler as not a monster,
but merely a human being, at the end confined in his
bunker, the last few days a defeated man, kind to his
female employees, tender to his new wife Eva Braun;
orders lapsed, with non-existing units into battle, humbly,
defeatedly declaring his beloved nation as unworthy ,
then quietly took his life; it dared proclaim

this monster who ordered the Holocaust and started
WW2 that killed fifty million people, as a hero larger
than life for standing firm until the end; that this was
not a monster... just a man... just a human being...

not a monster??? not a monster??? just a human being???

if he was just a human being, then we must all somehow
be monsters...